THE BOOKS OF THE PILGRIMS

Garland Reference Library of the Humanities (Vol. 13)

THE BOOKS OF THE PILGRIMS

by
LAWRENCE D. GELLER
M.A., F.P.S.
Director and Curator of Museum Collections
The Pilgrim Society

and

PETER J. GOMES
D.D., F.P.S.
Librarian of The Pilgrim Society
and Plummer Professor of
Christian Morals in Harvard University

GARLAND PUBLISHING, INC.
New York and London
1975

© 1975

By Lawrence D. Geller

Peter J. Gomes

Library of Congress Cataloging in Publication Data

Geller, Lawrence D
    The books of the Pilgrims.

    1. Bibliography--Rare books--Catalogs. 2. Pilgrim
Fathers--Libraries. 3. Pilgrim Society, Plymouth, Mass.
I. Gomes, Peter J., joint author. II. Title.
Z997.A1G44   016.09   74-30056
ISBN 0-8240-1065-5

Printed in the United States
of America

For The Rt. Rev. John K. Cavell, M. A., F.P.S.
and for The Rev. Robert Merrill Bartlett, D.D., F.P.S.

Men of letters and
Friends of the Pilgrims and their books

TABLE OF CONTENTS

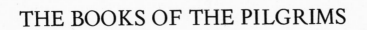

THE BOOKS OF THE PILGRIMS

PREFACE

It is not often that one thinks of the Pilgrims of Plymouth as literary figures. Books and letters seem a luxury in an enterprise whose first priority was basic survival and whose ultimate destiny was relative obscurity. The Protestant principle of *sola scriptura* as applied to the Pilgrim heirs of the Reformation suggests not only their overthrow of prelacy and tradition, but their meagre library as well. This view, like so many others about the Pilgrims, is clearly wrong and is not supported by the record available to us. The Pilgrim movement, like the larger Puritan movement of which it was but a part, expressed and maintained itself through books, the most essential of weapons in any intellectual arsenal. The Pilgrims and the Puritans were the lively heirs of three revolutionary traditions, the last of which, the Reformation, was made possible by the first two: the invention of the printing press and the translations into English of the Bible. By these three events, religious and intellectual controversy, long the preserve of clerics and scholars, became available to a wider constituency whose progeny extended to the shores of the New England wilderness in the first quarter of the 17th Century. Thus, the intellectual development of the Puritan movement, begun in Europe and England, was translated to New England where it provided the formative literary basis of the republic.

Considerable scholarly attention has been paid the major sources of the Puritan literature both in England and New England. From the Mathers to the heirs of Perry Miller has come an apparently endless bibliography on the subject. With the possible exception of William Bradford's *Of Plymouth Plantation,* however, the literary history of the Plymouth Pilgrims has been largely ignored. Two signal exceptions to such scholarly indifference appeared in the last years of the 19th century and the first years of the 20th century in the monumental works of Henry Martyn Dexter and Edward Arber, both stimulated in part by the "recovery" of the Bradford manuscript and its return to Massachusetts in 1896. One English and the other American, Arber and Dexter, through superb detective work, provided an incomparable literary history of the Pilgrim movement in Holland, England, and America. By their prodigious energies, unexcelled in their time or our own, the Pilgrims were liberated from the happy provincialism to which they had been consigned by a doting but uninformed public, and restored to their proper place in the post Reformation intellectual scheme.

Edward Arber (1836-1912), a self-made English scholar (he was for twenty-four years a clerk in the Admiralty) and Professor of English at Birmingham University from 1894 until his untimely death in 1912, was considered one of the most prolific editors and compilers of English literary texts of his generation. In 1897 he brought out a stout little volume entitled *The Story of the Pilgrim Fathers, 1606-1623 A.D. As Told By Themselves, Their Friends, and Their Enemies*, published simultaneously in London and Boston. Its 634 pages were designed to provide an "adequate account, scientifically written but popular in form, of the Pilgrim Fathers." With all of this, Arber's account extended but to the third year of the Plymouth Colony. "If that story is to be continued," he observed, "it must be in another similar volume; which would probably carry it on to the years 1628, or 1630." From 1903 until his death he was at work on such a second volume, conducting a lively international correspondence with his friend, Arthur Lord of Plymouth, noted Pilgrim Scholar and President of the Pilgrim Society. Arber was impressed by the need to recover what he styled "a lost literature." He wrote:

> It is extraordinary to what extent we are dealing in this volume with what is practically a lost literature. All the English books printed in Holland and Flanders before 1641 are rare; but those printed for the Separatists in order to be sold or distributed in England are amongst the rarest of them all. (Arber, p. 8)

He was distressed, for example, that the incomparable British Museum contained not a single copy of the original editions of the seven books written by the se-Baptist John Smith, printed for him between 1603 and 1613. Clearly, it was necessary to mount a great scholarly search for these and similar missing elements in the Separatist literature.

> Therefore we would here strenuously appeal to all the great collectors and libraries of the United States especially those in New England that instant search should be made through their collections for all the English Separatists works known . . . . And further that the finds should be reported to, and recorded by, some central body like the American Library Association.

This is not a sectional literature. It is that which surrounds the ultimate origin of the United States, and therefore the effort may be regarded as a national one. (Arber, p. 9)

Not many accepted Professor Arber's invitation, and indeed, after the publication of the *Pilgrim Press* (Cambridge, England, 1922) by Rendal Harris and Stephen K. Jones, a useful study identifying the books printed on the press of William Brewster at Leyden, little if any attention was paid the volumes with which Professor Arber was so much concerned.

Henry Martyn Dexter (1821-1890) was acknowledged as one of the most eminent scholars of the literature of New England, this no modest accolade to one who was the successor to Dr. Alexander Young and the colleague of Dr. Williston Walker. His great scholarly monument, *Congregationalism As Seen In Its Literature,* was published in 1880. It was impressive in scope and achievement, identifying the vast wealth of the "hidden literature" of Puritanism and locating extant volumes thereof in the libraries of the world by means of his Dexter numbers. The bibliography of Congregationalism, so notably begun by Dexter, was added to in 1893 by Yale's Williston Walker with the publication of his *Creeds and Platforms of Congregationalism* with its careful discussion and systematic analysis of the evolution of Congregational polity. Thus, by 1897, when Professor Edward Arber produced his volume, the intellectual legacy of the Pilgrims as seen in their literature had been under competent discussion for some time in New England. Of Dexter, Arber writes:

The Rev. Doctor Henry Martyn Dexter, of New Bedford, Massachusetts, a wealthy Congregational Minister, and a splendid Scholar and Researcher, has made the preparation of the present volume easier by his works; and especially by his *Congregationalism As Seen In Its Literature,* 1880. Perhaps no man has ever hunted more strenuously, or over as long a period of time, or more regardless of expense, after the ultimate facts of the Pilgrim story than Doctor Dexter has done. (Arber, p. 49.)

Dexter's greatest contribution to the literature of the Pilgrims, however, was to come in 1905 when he published together with Morton Dexter *The England and Holland Of The Pilgrims.* The books that the Pilgrims read, wrote, and debated were his chief concern, and through his exhaustive and exacting researches he produced as lively and complete an intellectual history of the Separatist movement as had ever been seen, and it has not been superceded. In terms of the history of the Pilgrims, an enterprise which had been well under way since at least Nathaniel Morton's authorized history of the colony in 1669, Dexter placed emphasis upon the rare literary remains of the Separatist movement in Holland and England and America. He exhumed the ancient volumes that recorded the early battles of Puritanism and made that lively era live again. He had long been interested in the bibliographical details of the Pilgrims, and, in 1889, communicated to the Proceedings of the Massachusetts Historical Society his paper on *Elder Brewster's Library*, "contained in the sworn inventory made 18-28 May, 1644, by Governor William Bradford, Assistant Thomas Prence, and the Reverend John Rayner and recorded in the Plymouth Colony 'Book of Wills' Vol. 1, p. 53-59." This interest he shared with Arthur Lord of the Pilgrim Society who in his own essay on the subject of Elder Brewster's books entitled "The First New England Library," wrote

> I have hoped to secure for the Pilgrim Society, to which has been entrusted the duty of securing and preserving those memorials of the Pilgrim days, which time and change have spared, a substantially complete set of all the books that once stood on the shelves of the Pilgrim Elder and which through his long life of usefulness and honor were both a solace and an inspiration, a dream not impossible of fulfillment. It may not be possible to recover the identical volumes whose pages he turned with proud care and bore the marks of his constant study for but few are known to have endured; but the editions which he studied, we know, from the great libraries of the old world and the new are today to be found copies of all the books enumerated in that minute inventory of 400 volumes . . . (unpublished manuscript Pilgrim Society Library)

In large measure, Lord was successful in his quest, and his personal library, given to the Pilgrim Society at his death in 1925, is in some respect a replica of that of Elder Brewster.

Since its founding in 1820, the Pilgrim Society has sought to preserve both the bibliographical treasures in its keeping and to make them available to a wider public. Mindful of that responsibility, we offer the present illustrated catalog of our rare books in the hope that these volumes may be both understood within their historical context and appreciated as a tangible link with the intellectual and spiritual ancestors of New England. In doing so, we acknowledge our great debt to our predecessors in the Library of the Society, and particularly to Miss Rose T. Briggs, Director Emerita, under whose administration the first short title catalog was prepared. We reserve our greatest gratitude to Henry Martyn Dexter, Edward Arber, and Arthur Lord, whose heirs we are, hoping with them that the publication of this catalog will encourage a new generation of scholars to continue this work so well begun so long ago.

> *Every other author may aspire to praise; the Bibliographer can only hope to escape reproach, and even this negative recompense has been yet granted to very few.*

Samuel Johnson

Pilgrim Hall
The Pilgrim Society
Plymouth, Massachusetts
25 November, 1974

Lawrence D. Geller, Director

Peter J. Gomes, Librarian

THEOLOGY AND HISTORY IN PILGRIM LITERATURE
TITLES BEFORE 1620
Part I

Some historians see history as progression towards a goal in the future. Some argue for a cyclical view of progression and return. There is little doubt that apart from a philosophy of the direction of the past, if indeed the past has had a direction, the writing of history is cyclical. In the third quarter of the 19th century and the early twentieth the great masters of Pilgrim historical research, Henry Martyn Dexter, Edward Arber, Champlin Burrage, F. J. Powicke, and W. H. Burgess, among others, concentrated their efforts on interpreting the religious climate of the late 16th and early 17th centuries. As such, they placed the Pilgrims, as Separatists, in the wider struggle of English Puritanism against the established church and constituted authority. Their field of research was intellectual and theological history, concentrated in England and Holland. The Tercentenary of the Landing of the Pilgrims in 1920 and the energy generated by that event produced numerous studies. It seems to have marked the apex in interest in the intellectual history of the Plymouth Pilgrims. For, in that year Walter H. Burgess's *John Robinson* was published by the Pilgrim Press and Arthur Lord's *Plymouth and The Pilgrims* by Houghton Mifflin & Company. That energy soon subsided and a lull occurred with a subsequent literary regeneration taking place about the mid-1950's with the researches of Samuel Eliot Morison. The literary products of the 1960's have turned their backs almost wholly on the intellectual side of the Pilgrim story and writing, and interest has focused itself about the economic life, political development, and the material culture of the Plymouth Colony. Only recently has there seemed to be an indication of a return to the intellectual history of Plymouth's beginnings, with the publication by the Pilgrim Press of Philadelphia of Robert M. Bartlett's *The Pilgrim Way*, a biography of John Robinson sponsored by the Pilgrim Society of Plymouth. This is the first significant history of the Pilgrim's religious leader in fifty years.

Shortly following the appearance of *The Pilgrim Way*, three important books were published which began to fulfill the need for a return to the intellectual history of Plymouth Colony. B. R. White's *The English Separatist Tradition from the Marian Martyrs to the Pilgrim Fathers* (Oxford, 1971), is by its title

1

self-explanatory. Harry Ward's *Statism in Plymouth Colony* (N. Y., 1973) is a judicious study of the relationship of the individual to the state in the colony's political affairs. Francis Dillon's, *A Place for Habitation, The Pilgrim Fathers and Their Quest* (London, 1973) put the Pilgrims within the Puritan movement as individuals who sought to find their place within the compromises of the Elizabethan Church and could not.

Research in the rare book collection of the Pilgrim Hall Library permits the scholar to put the movement of the late 16th century for separation from the Church of England into the entire theological context of the 16th and 17th centuries. It is possible to start with the opening gun of The Reformation, *A Commentary of Master Doctor Luther Upon The Epistle of St. Paul to the Galatians* and work into the great writers of the Swiss Reformation, John Calvin and The French Christian Humanist, Theodore Beza. The works of John Calvin cannot be omitted in any study of the theological ideas of the Pilgrims. Indeed, Calvin's *Institutes of The Christian Religion* profoundly affected the course of history. The influence of Calvin's thought upon John Robinson is a worthwhile subject for research. As J. T. McNeill indicates in his *History and Character of Calvinism*, (Oxford, 1954) 335-336.

> When Calvinism in early America is mentioned, thought turns naturally to the Plymouth and Massachusetts Bay Colonies. Different as these were, both were definitely Calvinist. The Pilgrim Fathers were loyal disciples of John Robinson, their Pastor at Leyden, whose counsel ruled their lives and solved their disagreements. R. G. Usher says, 'They no doubt followed Robinson in his espousal of conservative Calvinism, accepting fully the doctrine of the elect, of predestination, and all that that involved. They also championed the right of investigation in the scriptures for all individuals.'
>
> Robinson was a greater defender of ultra-Calvinist doctrines of the Synod of Dort. It is questionable how far any of the Pilgrims grasped the details of his theology, but they could not miss the un-Calvinist element of his church polity. They were Separatists on principle, who held the complete autonomy of the local church . . . . In this they were as far from the Calvinist model as were the Anglicans with their prayer book and

2

their prelates. Yet they were true Calvinists in their thoughts of God and conscience, and in their courage to live by their religion. The principles of mutual edification and fraternal correction which has been earnestly incalculated in the Reformed Churches entered into the habits of life in the Leyden congregation. When the Pilgrims formed their *Compact* and instituted their own government, they were following literally Robinson's advice given on their departure that they should elect to rule them 'such persons as do entirely love and will diligently promote the common good'—Phrases that might have come from one of Calvin's pre-election sermons . . . . It was reported that Robinson also charged them in these words:

'The Lord has more truth yet to break forth from his holy word. I cannot sufficiently bewail the condition of the Reformed Churches who are come to a period in religion and will go at present no further than the instruments of their reformation. Luther and Calvin were great and shining lights in their times, yet they penetrated not the whole counsel of God . . . Be ready to receive whatever truth shall be made known to you from the written word of God!'

Although, according to McNeil, Calvin might have accepted these words of Robinson as his own, he has gone too far in implying the same broad-minded liberality that was Robinson's to Calvin. Robinson could never have been responsible for the death of Spanish reforming theologian Miguel Servetus, nor could he bring himself to the dogmatism and rigidity of mind that was Calvin's. While Ozora Davis mentioned the extent of the intellectual and personal debt that Robinson owed William Perkins of Christ's College, Cambridge, no one has examined this relationship in depth. Robinson wrote and published a supplement to Perkins' The Foundation of The Christian Religion. The Pilgrim Society Library possesses this work as collected in the "Sermons" or "Works" of Perkins and a fruitful comparison might be drawn here. It is interesting to note that while Perkins could never go the whole route towards Separatism, it was in part the sermons of Perkins and the distillation of his thought that led Robinson to *The Justification of The Separation From the Church of England*

3

(1610). *The Justification* (two copies of which are in the possession of the Pilgrim Society) was perhaps Robinson's most significant work. It was directed against the Vicar of Workshop, Master Richard Bernard, a Cambridge Puritan who could not bring himself to separation and who had written a diatribe entitled *The Separatists Schism.* W. T. Burgess, in his biography of Robinson published in England in 1920, provides a remarkably germane discussion of Separatists church polity when he says,

> Put shortly, the main difference between Bernard and Robinson was about the nature and constitution of a true church according to the teachings of the New Testament. Robinson maintained that the authority for constituting a genuine Christian church and the pattern which such a church was to take in perpetuity were to be sought for in the Bible. He declared that the Church of England was not framed according to the model of the New Testament churches; consequently it was a duty to separate from it. The true church was constituted of those who make a voluntary profession of faith and separated themselves from the world into the fellowship of the gospel and the covenant of Abraham.' Robinson poured scorn upon the legal conditions for membership in the Anglican Church. 'A man,' he says, 'may go out of these countries (Holland) where I now live, as many do, and hire a house in any parish of the land and then become to the right of his house or farm, a member of the parish church where he dwells. Yea, though he have been nursled up all his life long in popery or atheism, and though he were formally neither of any church or religion; Yea, though he should profess that he did not look to be saved by Christ only and alone, but by his good meanings and well doings; Yea, if he will come and hear divine service, he is matter true as steel for your church; Yea, be he of the King's natural subjects he shall, by order of law, be made true matter of the church, whether he will or no.' To Robinson, this seemed to be putting the conditions of church membership on an entirely wrong footing. In his judgement, membership in a Christian church involved a definite personal responsibility in regard to matters of faith and conduct. Only those who made a voluntary profession

4

of Christian faith and undertook to follow a Christian way of life were fitted for the high privilege of membership in a Church of Christ. Any two or three making sincere professions of religion in this way could join together and so constitute a true church.

'This we hold and affirm' says Robinson, 'That a company consisting though but of two or three, separated from the world . . . and gathered into the name of Christ by a covenant made to walk in all the ways of God known unto them, is a church and so hath the whole power of Christ.' Judged by this standard, the parish assemblies in England were not churches at all.

The authority for church government lay not with Bishops and Archbishops or Presbytaries, but within the members themselves of the gathered churches. "This opinion," said Bernard, "is indeed the first A. B. C. of Brownism whereupon they build all the rest of their untruths. This is the ground of their outbreaking from all the churches in the world."

While many scholars have pointed to the social and moral reasons dividing the Ancient Brethren or the London Separatist Church and the Scrooby Fellowship which migrated to Amsterdam, little recent attention has been paid to the theological differences in opinion that separated the Separatists themselves. A better understanding of this neglected episode may be gained by a closer examination of Francis Johnson and Henry Ainsworth's *An Apology or Defense of Such True Christians as are called Brownists* (Leyden, 1604). It may serve to clarify this aspect while providing another explanation for the removal to Leyden of the Scrooby Congregation other than the sordid nature of the moral behavior of the Ancient Brethren as illustrated in George Willison's *Saints and Strangers* (1945) **See footnote.

Certain modern misconceptions exist among antiquarians and the untrained public concerning the Separatists' relationship to the Puritan movement. The word "Separatist" over the years has somehow become confused with Separatism from the Puritan movement rather than the more important separatism from the

** (George Johnson's *A Discourse of Some Troubles in the banished English Church at Amersterdam* (Amersterdam ? 1603) is the best contemporary document of the split among the Ancient Brethren. This seemingly unique copy is found in the Library of Trinity College, Cambridge.)

Anglican Communion. Generally speaking, there is a failure to realize that Separatism is Puritanism followed to its logical conclusion. Horton Davies in his *The Worship of The English Puritans,* (Glasgow, 1948) sums up substantially when he stated "In their nonconformity the radical Puritan had to accept the alternative either of Schism and Separation (following the examples of Penry, Barrow and Greenwood) or of suspension. As they could not bring themselves to deny that the Church of England was a true church and were unwilling to become Schismatics—the implications of Separatism—they remained within the fold of the church hopefully waiting for a change of heart in their leaders. Their witness was now expended in writing against the vestments and ceremonies and in putting forward their claims in the exercises known as 'prophesying.' Only a very small minority 'cut the painter' and became Separatists." An examination of the rare book holdings in the Pilgrim Society Library will point to the relations between Separatist and Puritan. Puritan and Separatist ideas were virtually identical in their desire first to return to the primitive church of the early Christian fathers. It was a question of emphasis and loyalty to the Church of England that differentiated the two. An examination of the rare book holdings of the Pilgrim Hall Library will indicate the proper position of Separatism as the left wing of the Puritan movement. Important Puritan (non-separating) tracts were the products of the Pilgrim Press in Leyden, and, eventually after settlement in North America, the ideas that originally spawned both Puritans and Separatists drew them closer together rather than further apart after 1630.

These books, and the other Brewster imprints (those books printed by Elder William Brewster at his press in Choir Ally in Leyden from 1617 to 1619) in the Pilgrim Hall collection, are priceless from the point of view of the historian and the collector. Edward Arber, F.S.A., in *The Story of The Pilgrim Fathers* (London, 1897) states,

> All the English books printed in Holland and Flanders before 1641 are rare; but those printed here for the Separatists in order to be sold or distributed in England are amongst the rarest of them all. One simple fact will be a sufficient illustration of this:
>
> The British Museum does not possess, at this moment of

writing, a single copy of the original editions of the seven books written by The Reverend John Smyth, the Se-Baptist, which were printed for him between 1603 and 1613. Of how many other English authors can it now be said that in their original editions they are totally unrepresented in the great London Library.

Therefore, we would here strenuously appeal to all the great collectors and libraries of the United States especially those in New England for all the English Separatist Works known. And, further, that the finds should be reported to, and recorded by, some central body like the American Library Association. This is not a sectional literature. It is that which surrounds the ultimate origin of the United States; and therefore the effort may be regarded as a national one.

Perhaps some of the most significant of the Pilgrim Society Library's holdings are the works of Thomas Cartwright, a Master of Arts of St. John's College, Cambridge, and later, Lady Margaret Professor of Divinity there. Master Cartwright was a radical Puritan who died in 1603, about the time that the Separatist congregations were forming. However, his writings had a strong influence upon the Separatists, especially the key figures in the movement. As early as 1582, Elizabethan Secretary Sir Francis Walshingham asked Cartwright to prepare a confutation of the Rhemist translation of the New Testament which had become part of the Catholic Douay Bible. Four years later in 1586, the work was nearly completed when Cartwright was forbidden by Archbishop John Whitgift to continue with his translation. Whitgift reasoned that Cartwright's translation would hurt rather than help the establishment due to the latter's well known Presbyterian views. One year before Cartwright's death, part of the work found its way into print through the services of the well known Puritan printer, Robert Waldegrave, who was at that time working in Scotland. However it was 1618 before *The Confutation of The Rhemists* was printed in full by the Brewster Press in Leyden. The work has been listed in a number of Pilgrim inventories indicating that Cartwright was rather widely read by the Pilgrims in America as well as in Holland. It, too, is part of the Pilgrim Hall collection.

Although the authorship of the controvertial, *An Admonition to the Parliament,* is uncertain, it seems very possible, due to

Cartwright's later strong and learned defense of the work, that he was its author, or, in part, responsible for it. This full statement of Puritan policy was an especially harsh attack on the pomp and idleness of the Bishops of the Church of England and was first printed by Thomas Wilcocks and John Field, staunch Presbyterians, in London in 1571. Cartwright was, at that time, in Geneva lecturing at the Academy headed by Theodore Beza, who was an admirer and friend as well as a theological ally of John Calvin. Beza's *Confessio Christianae Fidei*, (Geneva, 1577) is part of the Pilgrim Society Library Collection. It is possible that Cartwright got his manuscript back to London, if indeed he wrote it in the first place, in time for its 1571 publication. The Pilgrim Press republished *The Admonition* in 1617 in Leyden, and William Brewster was known to have owned this title, of which the Leyden edition is part of the Pilgrim Society Collection. Archbishop Whitgift immediately reacted to the original 1571 printing and retaliated with his *An Answere to a Certen Libel Intitled An Admonition to the Parliament* printed in 1571. (This book found a place in Brewster's personal library and now is part of the Pilgrim Society's collections). Cartwright's *A Reply to an Answer Made of Master Doctor Whitgift* resulted in his being deprived of his living. While a warrant was sworn out for his arrest in 1572, he fled to Germany, where his extended controversy with Whitgift continued. It was in Heidelberg, where Cartwright had become a student of the University there, that he translated into English, Walter Traver's *Ecclesiastical Discipline* which appeared under the title, *A Full and Plain Declaration of Ecclesiastical Discipline* (1574). Travers, an M.A. of Trinity College, Cambridge, had also studied with Beza in Geneva and it was here that the *Full and Plain Declaration* was written. Through the influence of Lord Burghley, Travers was made a reader at The Middle Temple and while there did much to bring Puritan ideas to the Inns of Court, which may account for the abundance of Puritan lawyers on the eve of the English Civil Wars.

The co-author of *Een Klare,* the Puritan minister Robert Cleaver, is also represented in the holding of the Pilgrim Society collection with his 1617 publication *A Brief Explanation of The Whole Book.*

One of the holdings among the many of the Pilgrim Society's collection, that had far ranging influence in the controversy between Puritan and Anglican, is the work of the Scottish Divine,

David Calderwood, *De Regimine Ecclesiae Scoticane Brevis Relatio.* It was a product of the Pilgrim Press in Leyden and was printed in 1618.

The General Assemblies of the Kirk of Scotland were the scenes of regular pitched battles between James I and the Scots. In the General Assembly that met at Perth from August 25th-27th, 1618, James was particularly aggressive in his attempts to force Episcopacy upon the unwilling Scots. Master David Calderwood then wrote his pamphlet called *Perth Assembly,* which was sent over to Leyden to be printed at the underground press of William Brewster in 1619. Concerning the printing of this famous pamphlet which eventually caused the search and seizure of the Brewster Press, Calderwood states in his *True History of the Church of Scotland,* published in 1678 and also a holding of the Pilgrim Society Library,

> "The same day, afternoon (Friday 11/21 June, 1619), after the King's letter was read in the Secret Council, (The Privy Council of Scotland at Edinburgh), the Captain of the Guard was directed immediately to search James Cathkin, Richard Lawson, and Andrew Hart, Booksellers (at Edinburgh), their booths and houses; for all writs (writings) books and pamphlets as it pleased them to call them, set forth against (the) Perth Assembly (of 25th-27 August 1618): and in special the book entitled *Perth Assembly* which was spread (distributed) in the beginning of June (1619). But neither the book, nor the author, Master David Calderwood was found . . . . The author of the book, from this time forth, removed from place to place, as the Lord provided for him, till the 27th of August (1619 O.S.); at which time he embarked and departed out of the country."

The Reverend Thomas Thomson's *Life of David Calderwood* in Volume VIII of the Woodrow Society's edition of Thomson's history tells that

> It was no easy matter to embody such a work in types, and bring it before the eyes of the Scottish public. And, therefore, it had to be printed in Holland; so anonymously withal, that it bore the name neither of author, printer, nor place of publication: And the copies were

9

smuggled over into Scotland, in April 1619, with great risk and difficulty—in short, the pamphlets were packed in vats; as if they had been a mercantile consignment of French wines or strong waters (brandy).

When they were landed at Burntisland, the Minister of the Parish, being a Prelatist, would fain have searched these suspicious looking commodities: but was only prevented by the accredited functionary of such inquests—the Collector of the Customs.

From Burntisland, these vats were brought to Leith: and while they lay upon the landing place, among other packages containing French articles of traffic, the sharp-eyed (John Spottiswood) Archbishop of St. Andrews passed by, and looked at them; but happily without suspicion.

But the matter and style of *Perth Assembly* betrayed its authorship: So the King and Bishops, in deep resentment, not only denounced the work as atrocious and seditious libel; but prosecuted the search after Calderwood more keenly than ever.

On this account, the house of James Cathkin (a distinguished bookseller in Edinburgh, and a well-known adherent of the Historian) was particularly suspected and carefully rummaged . . . Cathkin was groundlessly suspected of having printed the tract of the *Perth Assembly*; and, in consequence of this suspicion, he was apprehended in June 1619, at London; whither he had repaired in the course of his mercantile transactions.

He was examined by no less a personage than the august sovereign himself—
'Where were ye born?' demanded the King
'In the City of Edinburgh,' replied the bibliopole
'What religion are ye of? rejoined the King
'Of the religion your majesty professes,' said the bookseller
'The devil take you away, both body and soul! for you are none of my religion. You are a recusant. You go not to church.' Cathkin was then charged with having declared the Assembly of Perth to be unlawful. . and in allusion to the refusal of the Presbyterians to receive the

10

communion kneeling. The King said of the bookseller, still on his knees, 'See their people will kneel to me, and will not kneel to God' .... He was remanded to prison for further examination .... After a confinement of three weeks, he was set at liberty: As he made it evident that he had taken no part in the printing or sale of *Perth Assembly.*

Meanwhile, Calderwood had successfully made his escape to the Continent where he sought out his publishers at Leyden. It is here also that the Scottish Presbyterian Minister attended the services of the Pilgrim Congregation at their meetings at the Green Gate. Edward Winslow in his discussion of the ecclesiastical position of the Pilgrim church at Leyden, refers to Calderwood in his *Brief Narration of the True Grounds or Cause of the First Planting of New England* published in London in 1646. It is interesting to note that even as late as 1646 Winslow refused to admit that the Pilgrim Press had anything to do with the publishing of the *Perth Assembly.* His discussion implies ignorance of Calderwood and his publication ventures, even though this incognito text has been identified by Rendel Harris and S. K. Jones in their book, *The Pilgrim Press* (Cambridge, 1920), as definitely printed by Brewster and Winslow using as evidence a thorough study of comparative typography. Winslow says,

> That a godly divine (David Calderwood) coming over to Leyden in Holland where a book was printed, anno 1619, as I take it, showing the nullity of the Perth Assembly, whom we judged to be the author of it and who was hidden in Holland for a season, to avoid the rage of those evil times whose name I have forgotten. This man being very conversant with our Pastor, Master Robinson, and using to come to hear him on the Sabbath. After the sermon ended, the Church (being) to partake in the Lord's Supper this minister stood up and desired he might without offense stay and see the manner of his administration and of our participation in that Ordinance.

> To whom our Pastor answered in these very words, or to this effect: 'Reverend Sir, you may not only stay to behold us; but partake with us, if you please; for we acknowledge the churches of Scotland to be the churches of Christ.

11

The Minister also replied to this purpose, if not also in the same words: 'That, for his part he could comfortably partake with the church; and willingly would: but that it is possible some of his brethren of Scotland might take offense at his act; which he desired to avoid, in regard of the opinion the English churches (which they held communion withal) had of us. However, he rendered thanks to Master Robinson; and desired, in that respect to be only a spectator of us. . . .

This interchange, it is hoped, will finally settle the common misconception held by laymen that the Separatists, or the original Pilgrims of the Leyden Congregation, were somehow of a justly different theological hew than other Puritans. The theological distinction in the minds of many Americans between the Boston Puritans and the Plymouth Separatists, also has existed far too long. There were differences, to be sure, but they were differences of emphasis and were not major. Calderwood, a Scottish Presbyterian, indicates that he would have participated in the sacrament of the Lord's Supper with the Separatist Church with little theological queeziness, if it had not been for the fact that the Scottish Churches and the Anglican Churches were officially of the same communion, embodied under the leadership of James I and IV of England and Scotland. He, in doing so, might have embarrassed his Scottish brethren. Presbyterians, Quakers, Baptists, Congregationalists, and Separatists were all Puritans, a fact which scholars may find redundant, but nevertheless, needs to be said.

This essay has by no means explicated all the texts found in the rare book collection of Pilgrim Hall. It has attempted to deal with some of the books that were either printed and/or read by the Pilgrims. It has also attempted to set the Separatist movement, within the larger context of 16th and 17th Century English Puritanism by a look at its literature and some of the major personalities involved in this vital movement in the history of the western culture. As George Herbert said in the 17th century, "Religion stands tip-toe in our land, ready to pass to the American strand." The debates expounded within the pages of these rare editions were the matrices of a new American Civilization where there was more truth and light yet to come.

12

Theology and Literature in Pilgrim History
Titles After 1620
Part II

In the first portion of this essay, we have attempted to discuss the Plymouth Pilgrims in the light of the books which they owned and presumably read in both old and New England. In the remaining portion, we hope to discuss in some detail the books which the Pilgrims themselves produced and which are represented in various editions in the library of the Pilgrim Society at Plymouth.

Considerable research has gone into the study of the uses to which history was put and the purposes for which it was written by the 17th century American Puritans. It is remarkable indeed that history, one of the most ancient of the arts and a sign of civility and scholarship, should be the first product of the "howling wilderness" which was the New World. Neither the expected furs, the lumber, the fish, nor the animals was the major item of commerce between the old and new worlds; rather, history was the chief commodity. Of this, however, we should not be unduly surprised. The radical group of English Protestants who made the migration to the New World were acutely familiar with history. In a fashion they claimed themselves to be radically historical people, for it was history which engrafted them upon the world scene as distinguished and relevant players. This can be seen in what historian Peter Gay calls their "struggle for the Christian past." They did not look upon themselves as interruptors of the grand flow of Christianity, nor did they see themselves as innovators, a term they both feared and disliked. Rather, they claimed for themselves the preservation of the true genealogy. Their warrant was closest kin to the primitive churches and the New Testament models. The Romish Church, the Church of England, these were the usurpers of the rightful and lively heritage of the Gospel, and it was the responsibility of historically-read men to expose them for what they were. History, then, belonged to the Saints. History was a discipline for the Puritans which had ultimate purpose and meaning as a theological device.

Upon their arrival in the New World, the Puritans, rather than escaping from history, proposed to embrace it and redeem it, as well as make it. They were certain not only of the general utility of history, but they were convinced of the specific service it could

13

provide for them. As Kenneth Murdock suggests, "they looked on historiography not as a luxury but as a central support for their enterprise." (Kenneth B. Murdock, *Literature and Theology in Colonial New England,* Harvard, 1949, p.73.) To the support of this enterprise, therefore, the Puritans employed history to extol righteousness, denounce evil, defend the colonies against unjust or unfavorable criticism and comment, and justify their religious and political experiments in a land without precedent for either. Such a practice of history helped the Puritan to establish his identity in relationship to the traditions, symbols, myths, common experiences and common culture of the world far removed from his little province.

Consequently, history was not mere "facts" or happenings. History was a process to be exegeted and understood. And as the Puritans criticized the "dumb reading" of scripture as not being of sufficient edification, so too did they find that history must point beyond the thing in itself. For if the Puritan's belief that history was the tangible record of God's power in the world was correct, men must be told what that history meant in order that they might understand God's activity and the purpose of their own. Such salvation history is clearly in mind when Governor William Bradford records that he was filling in his history of Plymouth with circumstantial detail so that the children of the first comers "may see with what difficulties their fathers wrastled in going through these things in their first beginnings and how God brought them along not withstanding all their weaknesses and infirmities." (Peter Gay, *A Loss of Mastery,* Berkeley, 1966, p.146.) Such is also the purpose behind the famous remark of Urian Oakes when he noted that "it is our great duty to be the Lord's Remembrancers or Recorders." In this fashion, the Puritan history became not just that of a group of exiles in the second decade of the 17th century. Rather, it became the legitimate heir of all of God's activity since the creation. Their epic was of equal substance with that of the Children of Israel, with whom they loved to identify; God moved with equal ease from Eden and Genesis to Plymouth and Boston.

The participation of the Plymouth Pilgrims in this sense of the Puritan historiography is now the subject of our discussion. And our attention is directed to the historical offerings of that English decade from 1620 to 1630 at Plymouth. What prompted the Pilgrims in the midst of their very real vicissitudes to write

14

history? In 1622 a strange little volume appeared, the first native history concerning the Pilgrims. Published in London it was known as "Mourt's Relation" because of the absence of any apparent author and the signature below the Epistle Dedicatory which seemed to read "G. Mourt." In his preface, "Mourt" states his understanding of the voyage and settlement of Plymouth, namely the desire of bringing the Gospel of Christ to these foreign parts and the securing of a place of "quiet and comfortable" habitation among other inducements. He concludes his remarks by saying:

> My hearty prayer to God is that the event of his and all other honorable and honest undertakings, may be for the furtherance of the Kingdom of Christ, the enlarging of the bounds of our soverign Lord King James, and the good and profit of those who, either by purse or person or both are agents in the same. (Alexander Young, *Chronicles of the Pilgrim Fathers,* Boston, 1844, p. 113.)

Together with this preface is a letter believed to be in the hand of Robert Cushman, which testifies to the veracity of the account in the following words:

> As for this poor relation, I pray you to accept it as being writ by the several actors themselves, after their plaine and rude manner. Therefore, doubt nothing of the truth thereof. (Young, *Chronicles,* p. 115.)

Dr. Alexander Young in his Chronicles of the Pilgrim Fathers (Boston, 1844) suggests the "Mourt" is really an error and stands for "G", or George Morton, a brother-in-law of Governor Bradford who came over to Plymouth in July, 1623. He further notes that the phrase the "several actors themselves" suggests that the body of the material was written by men active in the Pilgrim experiment, men whom he believes to be Bradford and Winslow.

The contents of Mourt's Relation are such as to suggest that the first portion is a daily journal in the hand style of William Bradford, extending from the discovery of land by the Mayflower in November, 1620 to the re-election of John Carver as Governor in April of 1621. In addition to this part are four narratives by Edward Winslow which exhibit in detail the chief operations of the Colony down to the return of the Ship Fortune in December 1621.

15

Henry Martyn Dexter in his highly-annotated facsimile edition of 1865 suggests that these accounts of the new plantation were not intended for publication at all, a suggestion prompted by a passage from Edward Winslow's *Good Newes from New England* (1624) which says that it was not understood when these journals left the hands of their authors that they would be published. (Henry Martyn Dexter, *Mourt's Relation*, Boston, 1865, p. xviii.) "Mourt" and Cushman quite probably recognized a good thing and with the insistance of the Merchant Adventurers, the stock company which underwrote the Pilgrim adventure, saw to it that the story was published. And it was a good story: It had the drama of the new wilderness, and as an innocent day to day account of adventure and opportunity, it would serve well as an inducement to others yet in England to emigrate. Such communications proved that the colonists had not fallen off the edge of the world, but, in fact, were successfully taming the wilderness to the glory of God and the improvement of his majesty's dominions. But not only would these journals be an interesting attraction to prospective colonists from the old world, but as "Mourt" probably recognized, they would be of great value to those merchants who were expecting a return upon their investment, for they speak of the potential riches of the land. This could be a shrewd appeal to the sensitivities of those who, "either by purse or person," shared an interest in the venture. And the affirmation of loyalists purposes "for the enlarging of the bounds of our soverign Lord King James" should certainly be an assurance of the good faith of the Colony whose legal base to settle was at best somewhat questionable. The text of the famous Mayflower Compact is found in this journal, and as it was a quasi-legal document whose opening words acknowledged the Lordship of King James, it too would be a useful device in persuading even the most skeptical of government officials of the good intentions of the little band. As if to make sure, however, that the most positive possible impression would be had from these writings, the introduction alleged to be Cushman's cautions: "If it be deficient in any thing, it is their ignorance, that are better acquainted with planting then writing." (sic) (Dexter, p. xxxvii.)

In the publication of the journals under the name of "Mourt's Relation" we have an example of history used to advertise and justify the Pilgrim venture in America. It thus constitutes the first published account of the colony and is of extraordinary value because of the authors' intimate association with the colony. It is one of the first contributions to an American native historiography and as such, provides the framework out of which subsequent works, more avowedly didactic and assuredly intended for the public press, were to develop.

According to William T. Davis in his Introductory Essay to Bradford's *History of Plymouth Plantation* (New York: Scribner's, 1908), there were then seven extant copies of the first edition of Mourt's Relation, one of which is in Pilgrim Hall. Davis goes on to give us an account of entire or partial reprints. In 1624, John Smith abstracted portions of Mourt in his *Generall Historie;* in 1625 it was published in condensed form in *Pilgrims of Purchas,* and in 1802 in the same form in the *Collections of The Massachusetts Historical Society.* The portion omitted by Purchas was printed in the Historical Society *Collections* in 1822. In 1841, Dr. Alexander Young published the entire work in his *Chronicles.* In 1848 George B. Cheever also published a complete version, and in 1865 appeared Dr. Henry Martyn Dexter's facsimile edition. Professor Edward Arber in 1897 published a complete version in his *Story of The Pilgrim Fathers* (London, 1897.) To this accounting of W. T. Davis must be added the new complete edition of Professor Dwight Heath in 1963.

Edward Winslow, of whom we have spoken in connection with "Mourt's Relation," in 1624 published in London what might be termed a sequel to the Relation under the title *Good News from New England* (London, 1624). This work, better known simply as "Winslow's Relation" is addressed "To all well-willers and furtherers of Plantations in New England, especially to such as ever have or desire to assist the people of Plymouth in Their Just Proceedings . . . " (Young, *Chronicles,* p. 271). Its purpose, like that of "Mourt's Relation" is to be . . . "a true Relation of things very remarkable at the Plantation of Plymouth in New England. Showing the wondrous providence and goodness of God, in their preservation and continuance, being delivered from many apparent deaths and dangers."

It is not too difficult to imagine that "Mourt's Relation" had excited a certain interest on the part of Englishmen in the doings at Plymouth. The publishing of a sequel within two years' time suggests a more than casual interest in the venture. Winslow, however, did not address this work to the idle reader, but rather to

17

those whose interests needed cultivation: the merchant adventurers. As he says in the preface:

> I therefore think it but my duty to offer the view of our proceedings to your considerations, having to that end composed them together thus briefly, as you see . . . (Young, *Chronicles*, p. 270).

History as seen in *Winslow's Relation* is employed for the justification and advertisement of the colony. As such it becomes a self-conscious *Mourt's*. The Pilgrim History will soon take a more vigorous and apologetic stand against detractors.

Despite the efforts of Mourt and Winslow to present the Pilgrim venture in the best possible light to those in England, grave misunderstandings developed. The basis of the Pilgrim settlement was called into question and charges were levelled against the colony. These aspersions seem to be that:

(1) The Plymouth Church was founded as the result of a schism in the Scrooby-Leyden congregation of John Robinson;

(2) The Plymouth Church with its separatist polity subverted the other churches gathered in New England in 1630;

(3) The Plymouth Church was a rabid, schismatic, Brownist, Separationist Church which professed separation from all other churches on obedience to the Separationist views of their Leyden pastor, John Robinson;

(4) The Plymouth Church was guilty of intolerance.

These were serious charges, and were they to go unacknowledged and uncorrected, they would have a disastrous effect upon the colony. To defend the integrity and purpose of the colony with a refutation of these charges was a task placed upon the shoulders of the able Winslow. In 1646 appeared a scathing pamphlet entitled *Hypocrisie Unmasked: By a true Relation of the Proceedings of the Governor and Company of Massachusetts Against Samuel Gorton, (and his accomplices . . .)* (London, 1646). It will not serve our purpose to discuss in detail the Gorton affair. Our interest in *Hypocrisie Unmasked* is in the *Brief Narration* Occasioned by

> certain aspersions of the true grounds or cause of the first Planting of New England; the Precedent of their churches in the way and worship of God; their

18

Communion with the Reformed Churches; and their practice towards those that differ from them in matters of religion and church government.

To these charges Winslow responds, " . . . let me briefly answer some objections that I often meet withal against the country of New England." To the charge that the Plymouth congregation was gathered out of schism from the Scrooby-Leyden church, Winslow answers that nothing is more untrue. The reasons for separation raised by Pastor Robinson and Elder William Brewster were these: " . . . they thought we might more glorify God, do more good to our country, better provide for our posterity, and live to be more refreshed by our labours than ever we could do in Holland where we were." The lengthy argument concludes with an affirmation that there was no breach between the Leyden and Plymouth factions of the church. Between the two was no breach " . . . but such love as indeed is seldom found on the earth."

To the charge that the Plymouth congregation subverted the other churches of Massachusetts Bay by the separatist model which these newer churches were swift to follow, Winslow responds that the primitive and apostolic churches served as the model rather than the Plymouth congregation. All the other churches (Salem, 1629) had done was to search the scripture to see if the practice of Plymouth was thereby warranted. And finding that it was, they too adopted the same model. This argument concludes "So that here thou mayest see they set not the church at Plymouth before them for example, but the primitive churches were and are their and our mutual patterns and examples . . . " To the charge that the Plymouth congregation embraced absolute separation to the point of nonfellowship with other churches of New England, and that this was in response to the extreme teachings of their Pastor John Robinson, Winslow gives an account of the intellectual and spiritual pilgrimage of Robinson. He makes note of Robinson's earlier espousal of separatist principles and his later mellowing on the subject. In answer to this charge, Winslow recorded from memory the now-famous farewell address of Robinson to the Pilgrims in which he charged them in part that "The Lord hath more truth and light yet to break forth from out of his holy word." Their separation according to Winslow's account of Robinson's teachings was to be from the world and not from other churches. "tis true we profess and desire to practice a separation from the world, and the works of the world, which are the works of the flesh such as the Apostles speaketh of."

"The next aspersion cast upon us is, that we will not suffer any that differ from us never so little to reside or cohabit with us; no not the Presbyterian government which differeth so little from us. To which I answer our practice witnesseth the contrary." And so it does, the presence of Quakers, Anabaptists, Presbyterians, Church of England men in the Colony represents a liberality which is surprising for the times. It is explained by Winslow that tolerance is granted to those of tender conscience who see God's word in a different light than "we" as long as " . . . their walking is answerable to the rules of the gospel, by preserving peace and holding forth holiness in the conversations among men."

> This much I thought good to signify, because we of New England are said to be so often prepounded for an example. And if any will take us for a precedent, I desire they may really know what we do, rather than what others ignorantly or maliciously report of us, assuring myself that none will ever be losers by following us so far as we follow Christ.

And with this conclusion to "Hypocrisie Unmasked" ends with but one exception the primary historiographical materials of the Plymouth Colony: what the Pilgrims said about themselves. They entered upon the historical field as if by accident with the impulsive publication of "Mourt's Relation." They leave it with a ringing defense of their system against those who would cast aspersions upon their motives and methods. In this transition, can be observed the development of history from anecdotal chronology to intellectual weapon of defense and interpretation. It now becomes necessary to consider the major historical contribution of the colony in the hitherto unpublished work of its governor, William Bradford.

It has been suggested that an interest in the writing and study of history and biography is stimulated by periods of crisis. History and biography call to the present mind the virtues, accomplishments, sacrifices and heroes of an earlier time and charge the reader directly or indirectly to "measure up" to these great expectations and achievements. History and biography also serve as stable referents in seasons of transition and change, and, as such, they give the busy and frustrated participants in these changes and transitions much needed breathing space and perspective. Such a context of crisis occurs in New England with the so-called decline in the temperature of piety in the mid-17th century. The climate of the Half Way Covenant and its efforts to adjust piety to procreation provides us with a convenient historical watershed in a discussion of New England life, for by the mid-1660's, New Englanders were publicly concerned with the decline in zeal. The history they now wrote was used neither to advertise the beauties of their situation to England nor to defend the Colonies from unjust attack from abroad. The history which they once exported as a commodity they now applied to problems at home. Interpreted in terms of God's providence, history was employed as an incentive to righteousness, celebrating the heroes of the earliest days of the colony in order that their posterity might be stimulated to better serve God in their turn. The United Commissioners of the Colonies urged that the several histories be compiled as early as 1646 while some of the "first comers" were still alive. John Goodwin in his *Pilgrim Republic* tells us that the call was reissued with new urgency until Plymouth responded in 1667 with a request that her towns provide money to support such a venture. The General Court granted twenty-five pounds from the public treasury and in 1669 appeared *New England's Memorial: or A Brief Relation Of The Most Memorable and Remarkable Passages Of The Providence Of God, Manifested To The Planters Of New England In America; With Special Reference To The First Colony Thereof, Called New Plimouth . . . Published for the use and benefit of present and further generations by Nathaniel Morton, Secretary to The Court For The Jurisdiction Of New Plimouth.* (Cambridge, 1669).

Nathaniel Morton came to Plymouth in 1623 and grew to manhood in the family of his uncle, Governor William Bradford. In 1645, he assumed the office of Secretary to the Colony, a position which he filled until his death forty years later. In addition to such vital resources as were available to him by virtue of his office of Secretary and Custodian of the Colony's records and papers, he had full use of the manuscripts of his uncle. And perhaps of most significance in light of the earlier concern of the Commissioners, he had the opportunity to communicate with such "first comers" as John and Elizabeth Tilley Howland, John and Priscilla Mullins Alden, and Susanna Winslow, widow of one governor and mother of another. As John Goodwin remarks, with

21

these resources, " . . . a history of the greatest value was therefore to be expected from his faithful and industrious pen. It is truly astonishing that the meagre result should have satisfied either his patrons or himself." (Goodwin, *Pilgrim Republic*, Boston, 1888, p. xvii).

From the Preface to the first edition (1669) of *New England's Memorial* which is dedicated to the Right Worshipful Thomas Prince, Governor of New Plymouth, comes Morton's reason for writing:

> The consideration of the weight of duty that lieth upon us to commemorize to future generations the memorable passages of God's providence to us and our predecessors in the beginning of this plantation hath wrought in me a restlessness of spirit, and earnest desire, that something might be achieved in that behalf, more (or at least otherwise) than as yet hath done.

And in his following Address to The Christian Reader, he observes:

> So then, gentle reader, thou mayest take notice, that the main ends of publishing this small history, is that God may have his due praise, his servants, the instruments, have their names embalmed, and the present and future ages may have the fruit and benefit of God's great work, in the relation of the first planting in New England.

And finally, writing in 1680 in a preface to the records of the First Church at Plymouth of which he was also custodian, Secretary Morton comments on his efforts of 1669:

> Some years since it pleased God to put an impulse upon my spirit to do something in a historical way concerning New England, more especially with respect to the Colony of New Plymouth; which was entitled New England's Memorial; in which I occasionally took notice of God's great and gracious work in erecting so many churches of Christ in this wilderness.

In all of these statements concerning the impulse to publication, we find the native antecedents of that historical form which would be later called the Jeremaid. It was Morton's task to remember the fathers and impart to their posterity a challenge to carry on the work. The *Memorial* itself enjoyed a wide popularity in its day and well it should. The chief basis of its fame and popularity was Morton's use of the papers and manuscripts of his late Uncle, Governor Bradford. Morton was no plagerizer, and he admitted with candor his borrowings from his famous uncle. And he himself suggests that a better work might have been the result had Uncle William lived long enough to pen and publish it himself.

Our interest in Secretary Morton is two-fold: He is our first "professional" historian. He is a dealer in secondary sources and as such cannot be considered a member of the first generation of Plymouth writers. And his history is the first Old Colony history which was designed chiefly for domestic consumption. Secondly, we are not only interested in the Secretary but indebted to him for his introduction of the historical work of his uncle to us. In the absence of the Bradford history (which at that time was a private and unpublished manuscript), the Memorial was a necessary and useful book. With the discovery of the Bradford manuscript, however, the Memorial is revealed to be a somewhat inelegant paraphrase and summary. To have read Morton and then to read Bradford is to be convinced of the justice of John Goodwin's "verdict."

There have been many editions of Morton's *Memorial* following the first publication at Cambridge in 1669, and this can be understood by virtue of its significance in lieu of the missing Bradford *History*. A second edition published in Boston in 1721 with a supplement by Josiah Cotton; the third appeared at Newport in 1772, a reprint of the Boston 1721 edition. 1826 saw two editions, one by Allen Danforth, a Plymouth printer and newspaperman, and the other, the long-awaited "Fifth" edition of Judge John Davis at Boston. A fascinating account of the mystery surrounding this edition of the *Memorial* is found in an essay by Albert Matthews in the Publications of the Colonial Society of Massachusetts, Vol. XIV (1914) entitled "A Ghost Book." The next year in that series of Colonial Society Publications, Arthur Lord continues to discuss the relationship of Judge Davis, The First Parish in Plymouth, and the Pilgrim Society in the publication of the 1826 "fifth" edition. In 1855 the Congregational Board of Publication published the *Memorial* together with other matters, and in 1903, the Club of Odd Volumes produced an edition with an introduction by Arthur Lord. 1910 saw an English publication of the *Memorial* with an introduction by John Maesfield, and other American editions followed in 1912, 1919, and the most recent, a facsimile edition in 1937.

Of William Bradford, historians seem not to have had too much. Edmund Sears Morgan says that Bradford's History " . . . remains the outstanding piece of historical writing produced in the United States before Parkman." Harvey Wish suggests that "Bradford, more than other Puritans, practiced the scientific ideals set down by Thucydides in narrating the Peloponnesian War." Samuel Eliot Morison, to whom we are indebted for an excellent edition of the *History,* adjudges the Bradford *History* "incomparably the best of New England colonial histories." And Peter Gay, who calls Bradford a "Caesar In The Wilderness," writes "The Theme is intricate, moving, and at times majestic, and Bradford rises to it in all respects; his book, unique in the rank of Puritan historiography, is an authentic masterpiece. Its limitations are the limitations of Puritan culture, its merits are its own."

It is an historical paradox that Bradford, perhaps our first historian in the full sense of the word, was, through a series of misadventures one of the last to be discovered and explored. His journal was a private affair, although parts of it were employed in *Mourt's Relation* and the Winslow Journal; and in spite of the fact that his well-intentioned nephew Nathaniel Morton copied or paraphrased passages from the Journal into the *Memorial,* the Bradford manuscript escaped the public domain though frequently consulted by such New England literati as Hubbard, Mather, and Prince. It was from the library of the former that the manuscript was lost, turning up nearly a century later in the library of the Bishop of London at Fulham Palace. Its return to the United States in 1896 was a welcome one and it was placed in the archives of the Commonwealth at the State House in Boston. Some had hoped that the volume would be returned to the Old Colony itself and placed in the Library of the Pilgrim Society. It was felt, however, that the Commonwealth was indeed the legal successor to the Plymouth Colony and that such a significant portion of the Commonwealth's history ought to be available at the present seat of the government.

Nearly fifty-five years prior to the return, however, the Massachusetts Historical Society published the Bradford Manuscript under the direction of Charles Deane, then its secretary.

Since that time, there have been six major editions. The two modern editions most frequently consulted are those of Worthington C. Ford (1912) and Samuel Eliot Morison (1952). A discussion of the variant editions would in itself be a fruitful enterprise, but the present concern is more properly directed to this: what makes the Bradford history so interesting?

Professor Peter Gay in his *A Loss of Mastery* places *Of Plymouth Plantation* unmistakably in the Augustinian tradition of Church History. This was a portion of the Protestant effort to identify solidly with the Christian past by certifying as it were the historical genealogy and credentials of the Reformation. And although *Of Plymouth Plantation* is a work of contemporary history, it nonetheless sees the pedigree of the Plymouth venture in the Biblical saga, the apostolic and primitive churches, the far-off precursors of the Reformation such as Wycliff and Hus, and of course, the works of Luther, Calvin, Zwingli, Ames, Robinson, and Bullinger, all of which are represented in Pilgrim inventories and discussed earlier in this essay. This parochial Protestantism cast the modest Pilgrim venture into the scope of cosmic history while, at the same time, it caused all cosmic history to find its nadir in that same modest venture. Such was the work of the Christian historian and his attempt to reclaim and redeem the past for his own purposes.

Bradford's use of history places him in a unique position in our discussion of historiography. Although he was keenly a Christian historian, that is one who saw his enterprise in terms of God's history and plan of salvation, his history is written neither to advertise the benefits of that enterprise to outsiders nor to bring up short a generation of laggards. His history is written in the confidence of one who views both success and adversity as signs of God's contemporary activity. God not only acted in the past, he is acting today to bring about what is. Bradford had little need to belabor the doctrine of Providence. It was a concept so intimate, so much a part of the make-up of that first generation of Saints as to be indistinguishable from their totality. We can observe that it is a generation unsure and unconvinced of God's continuous active presence that constantly seeks demonstrations of God's activity. The question of Providence in Bradford is integral to the whole fabric. While the question of Providence in Morton's *Memorial* is profoundly self-conscious, the confidence of Bradford is part of his charm and his power.

The *History* of Bradford extends only to 1646, but it is clear that he had intention of carrying it on. It should be remembered, however, that not all of Bradford's literary and historical energies were confined to the *History*. John Goodwin tells us that he was a prolific letter writer. His extant letters move with the same grace and candor of the *History,* and fortunately some of them can be seen in the so-called Letter Book at the Massachusetts Historical Society. He was a student of Latin and Greek, and later on in life turned to the study of Hebrew. His efforts at Hebrew are discussed by Isidore S. Meyer in an article entitled "Hebrew Preface to Governor Bradford's History of the Plymouth Plantation" (Publications of the American Jewish Historical Society, No. XXXVIII, part 4, June 1959). This work was reprinted by the Pilgrim Society in 1974 under the title of *The Hebrew Exercises of Governor William Bradford.*

By far the most interesting work from the hand of Governor Bradford, apart from the *History,* is his "A Dialogue, or The Sum Of A Conference Between Some Young Men Born in New England and Sundry Ancient Men That Came Out Of Holland And Old England, Anno Domini 1648." The original holograph copy of this work in Bradford's own hand with his Hebrew characters on the cover and interleaved throughout, is in the Library of the Pilgrim Society. The "Dialogue" was composed two years before the end of the *History,* and, quite frankly, seeks to bridge what we could now call a "generation gap." The publication of the Dialogue was first made by Dr. Alexander Young in his *Chronicles* (1844), having discovered them written into the records of the First Church by Nathaniel Morton. Morton's preface states the case:

> I have lately met with a plain, well composed, and useful Dialogue, penned by that honored pattern of piety, William Bradford, Esq., late Governor of the Jurisdiction of New Plymouth Colony which occasionally treats something of this matter; together with and in defense of such as I may without just offence term martyrs of Jesus, and in defense of the cause they suffered for; it being no other in effect but what our church and the churches of Christ in New England do both profess and practice.

(In 1855, the Congregational Board of Publication also published the *Dialogue* together with an edition of *New England's Me-*

morial.) The holograph copy in Pilgrim Hall is there on loan from the Massachusetts Historical Society who themselves received it as follows:

> Jan 7, 1826. This also was found among some old papers taken from the remains of Rev. Mr. Prince's collection, belonging to Old South Church in Boston, and by consent deposited in library of the Massachusetts Historical Society.
>
> A(lden) Bradford.

It has been in Pilgrim Hall since the mid-19th century and has recently been restored by the New England Document Conservation Center in North Andover, Massachusetts.

Although certainly not of his authorship, another volume intimately associated with William Bradford is his edition of the so-called "Breeches Bible" which is in the Library of the Pilgrim Society. It is a small quarto measuring on the leaves eight by six and a half inches, and has the original calf binding, whole but somewhat broken. Most of the pages are intact with the exception of the title page which, until the mid-19th century, carried the Governor's autograph. Bradford genealogical data is to be found on many of the pages. It appears to have been handed down from father to son until the 18th century when it entered into a femal line. Alice Bradford, great-granddaughter of the Governor, married a Zebulon Waters and the Bible was in the possession of the heirs of that marriage until 1903 when it was presented by them to the Pilgrim Society Library. Called the "Breeches Bible" because of its quaint rendering of "breeches" for "Apron" in Genesis 3:7, the Bradford Bible is the Geneva edition of 1592. Bradford's copy provides for both a Concordance and an Apocrypha, but the Apocrypha is missing. It will be found that the scriptural references in Bradford's *History* and other writings conform to the translation of the Geneva edition rather than the "authorized" or King James version of 1611.

The catalogue of rare books in Pilgrim history, to which this essay is intended as a helpful introduction, should provide a sampling of the books which the inhabitants of Plymouth colony both read and wrote. It should also put to rest the notion that the Plymouth Pilgrims had neither time nor aptitude for books and the life of the mind. To be sure, the settlers of Plymouth, in Thomas Goddard Wright's words, were "mostly village and country folk of no particular education," and that "prior to 1650 Harvard College neither received from Plymouth nor contributed to that place more than one or two persons." (Thomas Goddard Wright, *Literary Culture In Early New England*, Yale, 1920, p. 15). And yet, as Wright goes on to say, "Very few of the Pilgrims were without books." (p. 27). Authoritative evidence for this conclusion is found in the *Wills and Inventories of Plymouth Colony*, published with painstaking care by George Ernest Bowman in the "Mayflower Descendant" and analyzed with equal care by Rose T. Briggs and Richard B. Bailey on behalf of the Pilgrim Society and Plimoth Plantation, Inc. According to Wright, "Of over seventy inventories examined in the first two volumes of the Wills, only a dozen failed to make specific mention of books . . . " (p. 27). Rose T. Briggs tells us that between 1633 and 1640, twenty-one inventories were filed with the General Court of Plymouth Colony, eleven of which mention books: 17 bibles, 6 psalters, and 85 other titles. The largest library in this period is that of Dr. Samuel Fuller, the Pilgrim physician. Of those inventories filed between 1640 and 1650, Elder Brewster's is the largest and best known, due in large measure to the work of Henry Martyn Dexter. Many of the books in his inventory (some of which he produced on his own press) are represented in this catalogue. Governor Bradford's Inventory indicates a library of about eighty volumes including two bibles, one of which we have previously discussed. Many of his books were in Greek, Latin, Dutch; and the Hebrew which he was struggling to learn is represented by a Hebrew grammar. Examination of the titles in the inventories and the publication dates will indicate that the Pilgrims did not bring all of their reading matter with them on the Mayflower. Books appeared, even in this remote region, not long after publication and were utilized by their owners. Says Wright, "It is evident that even in Plymouth, which had no bookseller, and was in general far behind Boston in culture, books fresh from the press were not unknown." (p. 59).

The intellectual life of Plymouth in the 17th century had a quality which might be called surprising endurance. That "mostly village and country folk of no particular education" could sustain such a life as represented by these books which they read and wrote is a testimony to the persistence of the life of the mind in even so inhospitable a clime as this.

1490?		EXPOSITIONES SIVE DECLARA–TIONES . . .
. . .	Somner, William	GAVELKYND (no title-page or date; pp after 160 missing. Cover, brittle vellum. In box with GAVELKYND is an article re Manor of East Greenwich)
1531	Zenophon	ZENOPHON . . . HAGANOAE, PER JOHANNEM SECERIUM . . . M.D. XXXI
1557* Basil	Moesel, Wolfgang	IN ISIAM COMMENTARIES . . . WOLFGANGUM MUSCULUM . . . BESILEAE . . . Belonged to Francis Bryan *Elder Brewster had this title in his library of 400 volumes inventoried in (Dexter #16) (folio)
1559 Rome		PRIVILEGIA AUCTO . . . (5-1/2" x 7-1/2"; vellum. Acces. #839)
1563 Geneva	Calvin, John	Joanis Calvini, PRAELECTIONES: IN LIBRUM PROPHRTIARUM JEREMIAE ET LAMENTRTIONES (Brewster had Daniel, Ezekiel, Isaiah)
1572*	Whitgift, John	AN ANSWERE TO A CERTEN LIBEL INTITULED, AN ADMONITION TO THE PARLIAMENT *Elder Brewster had this title in his collection (Dexter #199)
1573	Eckens, John	ENCHIRIDION LOCORUM COMMUNIUM ADVERSUS LUTHERUM . . .
1577*	Beza, Theodore	CONFESSIO CHRISTIANAE FIDEI . . . *Elder Brewster had this title (Dexter #45)

1580* London	Tromelius and Junius trans.	TESTAMENTI VETERIS BIBLIA SACRA . . . EXCUDEBAT HENRICUS MIDDLETONUS *Brewster had this title* (Dexter #10) Belonged to William Malcolm, 1699 Given by Miss Rose Whiting
Paris	Seneca	L. ANNAEI SENECAE PHILOSOPHI SCRIPTA . . . (Inscript. in Latin, indicating that the book belonged to the Jesuit College in Quebec, 1952
1592		THE GREAT ABRIDGEMENT OF ALL THE STATUTES OF ENGLAND . . . No author publisher, or date, but a note on the back of the title page is dated 1592
1592* London		BIBLE . . . IMPRINTED AT LONDON, BY THE DEPUTIES OF CHRISTOPHER BARKER *Belonged to Gov. Wm. Bradford* see C. Forman, "FOUR BIBLES IN PILGRIM HALL" in L. D. Geller (Ed) *They Knew They Were Pilgrims* (N.Y. 1971)
1592	Lambard, W.	EIRENARCHA: OR THE OFFICE OF THE JUSTICES OF PEACE . . . BY WILLIAM LAMBARD OF LINCOLNES INNE, GENT . . . Belonged to the Trial Justices of Plymouth, Mass. Given by Arthur Lord to the Pilgrim Society. Bears seal of the Cecil family. The Garter surrounding seal is that of the Knights of the Garter. Believed by Arthur Lord to have belonged to William Cecil, Lord Burghley and to have been given to William Brewster by Burghley. See L. D. Geller *The Arthur Lord Collection in the Pilgrim Hall Library* (Plymouth, The Pilgrim Society, 1971)

1596	Aristotle	No title page; several pages missing. On another page, the title is given as CIVIL GOVERNMENT. Bound in vellum. Given by Miss Sybil White of Marshfield, 1854
1597 Rome	Bosio, Jacomo trad.	GLI STATUTI DELLA SACRA RE- LIGIONE DIS. GIO. GIEROSOL IMITANO . . . (velum; damaged)
1599		THE BIBLE, THAT IS THE HOLY SCRIPTURES . . . London . . . Dep- uties of Christopher Barker . . . Gen- eva version; illus. Latin type. See "FOUR BIBLES IN PILGRIM HALL." Cited above. (Acc. no. 130) Purchased in London, 1866
1600*	Perkins, William	"Sermons" or "Works"; title-page and up to "C2" is missing. Contains: OF SALVATION AND DAMNA- TION . . . AN EXPOSITION OF THE SYMBOLE OR CREDE OF THE APOSTLES . . . PRINTED BY JOHN LEGAT PRINTER TO THE UNIVERSITY OF CAMBRIDGE AN EXPOSITION OF THE LORDS PRAYER . . . PRINTED FOR JOHN PORTER AND RALPH JACKSON A CASE OF CONSCIENCE . . . PRINTED FOR THOMAS MAN AND JOHN PORTER A DIRECTION FOR GOVERN- MENT OF THE TONGUE . . . PRINTED BY JOHN LEGAT TWO TREATIES . . . PRINTED BY JOHN LEGAT A DECLARATION OF THE TRUE MANNER OF KNOWING CHRIST CRUCIFIED . . . PRINTED BY JOHN LEGAT *A REFORMED CATHOLIKE: OR

A DECLARATION SHOWING
HOW NEERE WE MAY COME
TO THE PRESENT CHURCH OF
ROME . . . AND WHERIN WE
MUST FOREVER DEPART FROM
THEM . . . PRINTED BY JOHN
LEGAT . . .
THE FOUNDATION OF CHRIS-
TIAN RELIGION . . . PRINTED
FOR I.L. AND I.P.
On the title-page is written "John
Robinson's Book." It is not in a 17th
cent. handwriting. Folio: brass bound:
Stamped 1600 on the brass plate.
Repaired

NOTE: Pilgrim Hall has another copy
of the above sermons, pub. 1612,
q.v.
*Brewster had 2 vols. of Perkins'
Works (Dexter #80) and a separate
copy of A REFORMED CATHOLIKE
(Dexter #254)
*William Bradford, Ann Atwood,
and John Hazel all owned sermons by
Wm. Perkins (see Plymouth Colony
Wills and Inventories)

1602	Sternhold
London	&
printed	Hopkins
by	
John	
Windet	
for the	
assignes	
of	
Richard	
Daye	

THE WHOLE BOOK OF PSALMS,
INTO ENGLISH MEETRE
6-1/2" x 8-5/8"; rebound. The title-
page has a woodcut of Christ rising
from grave. The same cut appears in
the ed. printed for The Companie of
Stationers 1609, bound w. BIBLE,
L/A4/3. Decorative heading appear-
ing over "To the Reader" is the same
used by Brewster in his ed. of Cartwright's CONFUTATION, and in several other publications by various
printers. Two BULLS with sweeping
horns form part of this decoration.

1604*	(F. Johnson & H. Ainsworth)	AN APOLOGIE OR DEFENSE OF SUCH TRUE CHRISTIANS AS ARE . . . CALLED BROWNISTS . . . 1604 (bound pamph 5-1/4" x 7-1/4") *Brewster owned this title (Dexter) #282)
1605	Sandys, Sir Edwin	A RELATION OF THE STATE OF RELIGION . . . PRINTED FOR SIMON WATERSON
1608 London Robt. Barker		BIBLE . . . (NEW TESTAMENT 1610) (Black-letter) bound with CONCORDANCE . . . by R. F. H. and PSALMES . . . AND OTHERS . . . BY THOMAS STERNHOLD, JOHN HOPKINS . . . AND OTHERS . . . LONDON 1609 See FOUR BIBLES IN PILGRIM HALL
1608 London Robt. Barker 1609 Companie of Stationers		BIBLE . . . (blackletter) bound with
1609	Pulton, Ferdinando	DE PAGE REGIS . . .
1610*	Robinson, John	A JUSTIFICATION OF SEPARA- TION FROM THE CHURCH OF ENGLAND . . . BY JOHN ROBIN- SON . . . Belonged to Gov. Bradford, and has his signature. Brewster also had this title (Dexter #165)
1610	Robinson, John	another copy of the above, bound in battered and brittle vellum but re- cently restored
1611* London	R. G. (Richard Greenham)	THE WORKS OF . . . MASTER RICHARD GREENHAM . . . *said to have belonged to William White, Mayflower passenger. Brewster also had this title (Dexter #165) so did

Dr. Samuel Fuller and Deacon William Wright

1612*   Ainsworth, Henry
Amsterdam

BOOK OF PSALMES: ENGLISHED
BOTH IN PROSE AND METER . . .
BY H.A. . . . IMPRINTED AT AM-
STERDAM, BY GILES THORP . . .
1612 bound with:
TWO RIGHT PROFITABLE &
FRUITFUL CONCORDANCES . . .
COLLECTED BY RFH . . . IM-
PRINTED AT LONDON BY BON-
HAM NORTON AND JOHN BILL . . .
1622
Brewster had Ainsworth's PSALMES
(Dexter #76)

1612*   Perkins, Wm.
London
Legatt

"Sermons" or "Works." No title-page;
up to p. 113 missing. Consists of:
. . . SALVATION AND DAMNATION
AN EXPOSITION OF THE CREEDE
AN EXPOSITION OF THE LORDS
PRAYER A TREATISE TENDING
UNTO A DECLARATION,
    WHETHER A MAN BE IN THE
    ESTATE OF DAMNATION OR
    IN THE ESTATE OF GRACE
A DIRECTION FOR THE GOVERN-
    MENT OF THE TONGUE ACCOR
    ING TO GODS WORD
TWO TREASTISES:
    I.   OF THE NATURE AND
          PRACTICE OF REPENTENC
    II.   OF THE COMBAT OF THE
          FLESH AND SPIRIT
HOW TO LIVE AND THAT WELL
A SALVE FOR A SICKE MAN (THE
    RIGHT WAY OF DYING WELL)
A DISCOURSE OF CONSCIENCE
A REFORMED CATHOLICKE . . .
A DECLARATION OF THE TRUE
    MANNER OF KNOWING CHRIST
    CRUCIFIED

THE TRUE GAINE . . .
A WARNING AGAINST THE
    IDOLATRIE OF THE LAST TIMES
*Brewster and several others had
Perkins' WORKS; see note on the
edition of 1600
This copy was given to the Pilgrim
    Society by George W. Briggs,
    Assistant minister of the First Church
    1838-1853
It had belonged to James Perkins,
Esther Perkins and others. On the back
cover is a list of various Perkinses:
John, Esther, Edmund, James, Samuel,–
"the names of the children of the house"

1613	Pareus, David	EPISTOLAN AD GALATAS . . . DAVIDI PAREI Brewster owned IN HOSEAM and others Given by Asa Millet
1614* London Stansby	Seneca trans. T. Lodge	THE WORKS BOTH MORRALL AND NATURAL OF LUCIUS ANNAEUS SENECA . . . Belonged to Elder Brewster: Dexter #96
1615	Ames, William	SECOND MANUDUCTION FOR MR. ROBINSON (See Dexter, CONGREGATIONALISM)
1615	Cleaver	A BRIEFE EXPLANATION OF THE WHOLE BOOKE . . .
1615*	Dyke, Daniel	THE MYSTERY OF SELF- DECEIVING . . . OR DIS- COURSE AND DISCOVERY OF THE DECEITFULNESS OF MAN'S HEART *Brewster had this title (Dexter #167)
1617* Brewster Imprint		AN ADMONITION TO THE PARLIAMENT . . . Brewster re- printed THE ADMONITION TO THE PARLIAMENT, pub. by J. Field and T. Wilcox, London, 1571. Field

and Wilcox were Puritan ministers who were deprived of their rights to preach in their London churches. Brewster owned this title; Dexter (#18 thinks he had the London ed.

1617* Brewster Impr.	Dodd, John & Cleaver, Robert	EEN KLARE ENDE DUYDELIJCKE UYTLEGGINCHE OVER THIEN GHEBODEN . . . LEYDEN . . . VOOR BREWSTER BOECK*DRUCKER . . . 1617 Brewster owned this in English (Dexter # 176)
1617* Brewster Imprint	Ames, Wm.	GVIL. AMESII . . . RESCRIPTO . . . BREWSTERUM 1617
1617* Brewster Imprint		A FULL AND PLAINE DECLARA-TION OF ECCLESIASTICAL DISCIPLINE . . . 1617
1617* Brewster Imprint	Cartwright, T.	COMMENTARII . . . IN PROVERBIA SALOMONIS . . . AUTHORE THOMA CARTWRIGHTO . . . LUGFUNI BATAVORUM APUD GUILJEMUM BREWSTERUM . . . 1617 *Brewster had this title (Dexter #64)
1617	Cartwright, T.	Brewster imprint received July 26, 1965 (#1310)
1617 London	Purchas, Samuel	PURCHAS HIS PILGRIMAGE (in four parts-part 1) BY SAMUEL PURCHAS . . . (The heading over "To the Reader is the same which Brewster uses over "The Publisher to the Studious Reader" in his ed. of Cartwright's CONFUTATION, 1618. The design includes two BULLS with sweeping horns.
1617 London	Ravius	EPITHETO RUMIOAN . . . (back cover missing)

1617	Elton, Edward	AN EXPOSITION OF THE EPISTLE TO THE COLOSSIANS (notation on fly-leaf, "1741 November 9 then I began to read this book")
1618* Brewster Imprint		AN ABRIDGEMENT OF THE BOOKE WHICH THE MINISTERS OF LINCOLN . . . DELIVERED TO HIS MAJESTIE . . . *Brewster reprinted this pamph. and had a copy of it (Dexter #195)
1618* Brewster Imprint	Cartwright, T.	A CONFUTATION OF THE RHEMISTS TRANSLATION GLOSSES AND ANNOTATIONS ON THE NEW TESTAMENT . . . BY THOMAS CARTWRIGHT . . . PRINTED IN THE YEAR 1618 *Brewster (Dexter #83), Bradford, Jenny, Hazell all had this title)
1618* Brewster Imprint		A CONFUTATION OF THE RHEMISTS . . . . . *Another copy of the above
1618* Brewster Imprint	Cartwright, T.	CONFUTATION OF THE RHEMISTS TRANSLATION . . . *Another copy of the same work (Dexter #83)
1618* Brewster Imprint	Calderwood, D.	DE REGIMINE ECCLESIAE SCOTICANE BREVIS RELATIO . . . 1618
1619* Brewster Imprint	Calderwood, D.	PERTH ASSEMBLY . . .MDCXIX *Brewster printed this pamplet, and had a copy of it. (Dexter #186)
1619* et seq.	Ainsworth, Henry	ANNOTATIONS . . . (2 vols.) includes CANTICLES, PSALMES, DEUTERONOMY, NUMBERS, GENESIS, EXODUS, LEVITICUS Signature of Charles Chauncy, 1734 Also belonged to Israel Stoughton Moses Thompson, 1789

Moses Thompson, 1803
Given by Mrs. Nathan Fuller, Halifax
*Dr. Fuller, John Jenny,
R. Langford had this title

1619*   Ainsworth, Henry   ANNOTATIONS . . . includes:
                             DEUTERONOMIE   1619
                             NUMBERS   1619
                             PSALMES   1617
                             SONGS OF SONGS   1623

1620*   BIBLE . . . IMPRINTED AT LONDON
London   BY ROBERT BARKER, 1620
  and   with CONCORDANANCE, printed
1619   by Bonham Norton and John Bill, 1619
London   see FOUR BIBLES IN PILGRIM HALL
                             *This Bible belonged to John Alden

1619   SICILIA ANTIQUA
Leyden   PHILIPPI CLVVERI
                             (cover off; several pages missing)
                             . . . ex oficina Elseviriana . . .
                             MDCXIX
                             It is illus. with plates and maps, all
                             placed together, as in modern usage

1622   (Edw. Winslow   RELATION OF JOURNAL OF THE
London   &   BEGINNING AND PROCEEDINGS
         Wm. Bradford?)   OF THE ENGLISH PLANTATION
                             SETTLED AT PLIMOTH IN NEW
                             ENGLAND . . . PRINTED FOR
                             JOHN BELLAMIE . . . 1622
                             "Mourt's Relation," so called.

1622   Malynes, Gerard   LEX MARCATORIA OR THE
London   ANCIENT LAW MERCHANT . . .
                             (same title-page as . . . HISTORIE
                             OF ENGLAND . . . London 1626.
                             Title-page dec. like COLL. HIST.
                             ENG. (London 1625) with descrip-
                             tion of Scotland 1585. In Hudson's
                             edition of SHAKESPEARE'S
                             MACBETH p. XXI

38

1622* London	Elton, Edward	THE COMPLAINT OF A SANCTI- FIED SINNER ANSWERED (2nd ed.) (4°) *Brewster had this title (Dexter #128)
1624 London	White, John White, Francis	THE WORKES OF . . . JOHN WHITE . . . WITH A DEFENSE OF THE WAY TO THE TRUE CHURCH BY FRANCIS WHITE . . .
1625 Oxford	Goodwyn, Tho.	ROMANAE HISTORIAE . . . AN ENGLISH EXPOSITION OF ROMANE ANTIQUITIES . . . FOR THE USE OF ABINGDON SCHOOL
1625*	Robinson, John	OBSERVATIONS DIVINE AND MORRALL . . . BY JOHN ROBINSON . . .M.DC.XXV *Brewster had this title (Dexter #118)
1625	Minsheu, John	EMENDATP . . . MYNSHEUS AMENDS AND AUGUMENTATION FOR HIS GUIDE INTO THE TONGUES . . . (fol) (Minsheu was a professor of languages in London: see W. Somerset Maugham, DON FERNANDO
1626 London	Danyel, Samuel	THE COLLECTION OF THE HISTORIE OF ENGLAND (same title-page design as THE ANCIENT LAW MERCHANT above. THE DESCRIPTION OF SCOTLAND 1585 uses the same design. It is re- produced in MACBETH in THE NEW HUDSON SHAKESPEAR 1908) Belonged to Thomas Goodwin Nathaniel Goodwin, Beverly Given to Pilgrim Hall 1835 Has sticker of Gilchrist Circulating Library, London.
1628* Midelburge	Raleigh, Sir W.	THE PREROGATIVE OF PARLIA- MENTS . . . BY . . . SIR WALTER RALEIGH KNIGHT . . . PRINTED

		IN MIDELBURGE 1628 "John Robinson" on title-page; notes enclosed *re* this autograph. Conclusion, not the Pilgrim Pastor *Brewster owned this title (Dexter#277
(1628)*	Leighton, Alex.	AN APPEAL TO THE PARLIAMENT OR SIONS PLEA AGAINST THE PRELACIE . . . (the author was imprisoned, pilloried etc.) *Brewster had this title (Dexter #216)
1629*	Burton, Henry	BABEL NO BETHEL: THAT IS THE CHURCH OF ROME NO TRUE VISIBLE CHURCH OF CHRIST . . . *Brewster had this title (Dexter #343)
1629 London		SERMONS
l629 London	Paybody, Thomas	A JUST APOLOGIE FOR THE GESTURE OF KNEELING–IN THE ACT OF RECEIVING OF THE LORDS SUPPER . . . Belonged to Josiah Cotton, 1698/9
1629 London	Andrews, Lancelot	XCVI SERMONS . . . Belonged to Josiah Cotton
1631* London	Bolton, R.	A DISCOURSE ABOUT THE STATE OF TRUE HAPPINESS . . . (4°) Brewster had this title (Dexter #171)
1631	Rodrigvez, A.(S.J.)	THE TWO FIRST TREATISES OF THE FIRST PART OF CHRISTIAN PERFECTION TRANS . . . OUT OF SPANISH INTO ENGLISH (Lent by Rectory P. E. Church)
1632	Joannis Leonis Africani	AFRICAE
1632	Robinson, John	ESSAYES . . . . First posthumous edition. Robinson died in Leyden in 1625.

1633 Geneva	Pasor, George	LEXICON GRAECO-LATINUM IN N. TESTAMENTUM . . . Belonged to Josiah Cotton "given by my father 1693/94" Given by Mrs. Priscilla Cotton
1633	Ursinus, Z.	THE SUMME OF CHRISTIAN RELIGION. . . (printed by Robert Young) Given by Eunice D. Hedge
1635 London (?)		Pages up to 13 missing Acts of Parliament, from Henry III (printed in black-letter, by M. Flesher, I. Haviland, & R. Young, assigns of John More . . . "Bull" headpiece, c. f. Brewster Given by Mrs. LeBaron
1635 London	Pemble, Wm.	A PLEA FOR GRACE Belonged to John Cotton, Jr. Belonged to John Cotton Given by Thomas Bartlett
1635* London	Barriff, Wm.	MILITARY DISCIPLINE: OR THE YONG ARTILLERY MAN *Myles Standish had this title
1638 London	Robinson, John	ESSAYES . . . .
1635 London	Robinson, John	ESSAYES . . .
1638 Amsterdam Brewster Imprint	Cartwright, T.	COMMENTARII . . . IN PROVERBIA SALOMONIS (with a preface by Polyander) bound w. MELAPHRASIS ET HOMILIAE IN LIBRUM SALOMONIS "Brewster Bear" as colophon at end of preface and end of book. Binding damaged. Belonged to Joshua Moody 1687
1639	Ainsworth, Henry	ANNOTATIONS UPON THE FIVE BOOKS OF MOSES, THE BOOKE

41

		OF THE PSALMES, AND THE SONG OF SONGS OR CANTICLES . . . PRINTED BY M. PARSONS FOR JOHN BELLAMIE . . .
1639		BIBLE, KING JAMES VERSION
1640 London	Ovid	OVID'S METAMORPHOSIS ENGLISHED . . . BY G. S. (book-plate of the Right Honorable Charles Viscount Bruce of Ampthill)
1642		BIBLE
1642 London	Hildersam	LECTURES UPON PSALM LI Belonged to Jn° Cotton Given by Mrs. Priscilla Cotton
1642	Lechford, Thomas	PLAIN DEALING OR NEWS FROM NEW ENGLAND
1643 London		CHURCH GOVERNMENT & CHURCH COVENANT DISCUSSED IN AN ANSWER OF THE ELDERS OF THE SEVERAL CHURCHES IN NEW ENGLAND TO TWO AND THIRTY QUESTIONS SENT OVER TO THEM
1643 London	Prynne, Wm.	THE SOVERAIGNE POWER OF PARLIAMENTS AND KINGDOMS (belonged to Josiah Cotton 1713) (belonged to John Cushing 1732)
1644	Robinson, John	A JUST AND NECESSARY APOLOGIE OF CERTAIN CHRISTIAN . . . CALLED BROWNISTS . . . BY JOHN ROBINSON . . . M, FC, XLIII Published in English 19 years after the death of the Pilgrim's pastor in Leyden in 1625 First published in Latin in 1619.
1644 Cambridge	Burger, Franco	INSTITUTIONUM LOGICARUM LIBRI DUO Given by Mrs. Eunice D. Hedge

1645* London	Ursinus, Z.	THE SUMME OF CHRISTIAN RELIGION ... PRINTED BY JAMES YOUNG, 1645 (similar but not identical with ed. of Robert Young, London 1633 *Belonged to Josiah Winslow, son of the Pilgrim Edward Winslow and Governor of Plymouth during King Philip's War
1646	Winslow, Edw.	HYPOCRASIE UNMASKED ... WHEREUNTO IS ADDED A BRIEF NARRATION OF THE TRUE GROUNDS ... OF THE FIRST PLANTING OF NEW ENGLAND ... THE PRESIDENT OF THEIR CHURCHES IN THE ... WORSHIP OF GOD; AND THEIR PRACTICE TOWARD THOSE THAT DISSENT FROM THEM ... BY EDW. WINSLOW ... 1646
1646		THE TEXTS OF THE SEVERALS SERMONS Given by Mrs. Priscilla Cotton
1652 London	Williams, Roger	THE BLOODY TENENT YET MORE BLOODY BY R. WILLIAMS OF PROVIDENCE IN NEW ENGLAND
1652	Norton, John	No title page. Sermons Belonged to John Cushing 1730 Belonged to Josiah Cushing
1653 London	Gassendi, Petri	INSTITUTO ASTRONOMICA Belonged to Joseph Marsh 1730
1653		A PLATFORM OF CHURCH-DISCIPLINE ... AGREED UPON BY THE ELDERS AND MESSENGERS OF THE CHURCHES ASSEMBLED ... AT CAMBRIDGE IN NEW ENGLAND : AND REPRINTED IN LONDON FOR PETER COLE (foreword by Edw. Winslow)

1654 London	Brownlow, Rich.	DECLARATIONS COUNTS AND PLEADINGS . . . THE SECOND PART . . . (canvas cover) Belonged to Thomas Turner 1705 Belonged to John Cushing 1713
1654 London	Charleton, Walter	PHYSIOLOGIA Belonged to Henry, Duke of New Castle 1670 Belonged to Jn° Gardner 1732
1655	Sibbs	COMMENTARY OR EXPOSITION UPON . . . THE SECOND EPISTLE OF ST. PAUL TO THE CORRINTH- IANS (Uses "Bull" head-piece)
1655 London	Vane, Sir Henry	THE RETIRED MAN'S MEDITA- TION OF THE MYSTERY AND POWER OF GODLINESS (sold as dup. by "Aedea Christi. Acadamia Oxon)
1655	Trapp, John	MELLICUM THEOLOGICUM OR THE MARROW OF MANY GOOD AUTHORS bound with A COMMENTARY OR EXPOSI- TION ON THE GOSPEL ACCORD- ING TO ST. MATHEW followed by commentaries on the other books of the New Testament Title-page and front cover missing
1656 London	White, John	A COMMENTARY UPON THE THREE FIRST CHAPTERS OF . . . GENESIS
1656 London	Baxter, Rich.	THE REFORMED PASTOR . . . Belonged to Stephen Williams 1747 Belonged to Rev. Nathan Williams Tolland
1656 London	Harrington, J.	COMMON-WEALTH OF OCEANA Dedicated to HIS HIGHNESSE THE

		LORD PROTECTOR OF THE COM-MONWEALTH Belonged to Edward Winslow, an 18th century descendant of Governor Edward Winslow Colonial Advisor to Oliver Cromwell and a member of the Pilgrim Company
1658 London	C. B. and W. G.	DIVINE CHARACTERS IN TWO PARTS (has "Brewster Bear") Belonged to Jn° Cotton 1746
1659 London		A DECLARATION OF THE FAITH AND ORDER OWNED AND PRACTICED IN THE CONGREGATIONAL CHURCHES IN ENGLAND . . .
1659 London	(John Clark?)	FORMULAE ORATIONE IN USUM SCHOLARUM . . .
1659		A treatise concerning scandal
1661 Oxford	Lovell, Robt.	HISTORY OF ANIMALS AND MINERALS Belonged to John Wade, London, 1699 Belonged to N. Sever 1713 Given by Dr. J. B. Brewster, Plym. 1903
1662 London	Clarke	A COLLECTION OF THE LIVES OF TEN EMINENT DIVINES
1666 London	Caryl, Joseph	AN EXPOSITION . . . UPON THE 38, 39, 40, 41, 42 CHAPTERS OF THE BOOK OF JOB
1666 London	Wingate, E.	AN EXACT ABRIDGMENT OF ALL STATUES . . . FROM MAGNA CARTA UNTIL 1641 BY E. WINGATE OF GRAYES INN ESQ. . . . Belonged to Thomas Hinckley, last governor of Plymouth Colony
1668	Boroughs, Jeremiah	GOSPEL REMISS . . . (torn) OR A

	TREATISE SHEWING . . . TRUE BLESSEDNESS . . . (torn) CONSISTS IN PARDON OF SIN (given by Thomas Bartlett 1837)
1668 Elton, Richard London	THE COMPLEAT BODY OF THE ART MILITATY
1669 Walley Cambridge	BALM IN GILEAD . . . A SERMON BY THOMAS WALLEY . . . PREACHI BEFORE THE GENERAL COURT OF THE COLONY OF NEW PLYMOUTH . . . JUNE 1, 1669 CAMBRIDGE: PRINTED BY S. G. AND M. F. 1669
1669 Morton, Nath. Cambridge	NEW-ENGLAND'S MEMORIALL . . . BY NATHANIEL MORTON . . . CAMBRIDGE . . . 1669 (S.G. and M.F
1669 Morton, Nath. Cambridge	Another copy of the above; broken binding
1669 Morton, Nath. Cambridge	Another copy of the above; rebound
1669 Leger, Jean Leyden	HISTOIRE . . . DE . . . VAUDUIS PAR JEAN LEGER PASTEUR & MODERATEUR DES EGLISES DES VALLEES, & DEPUIS . . . LA PERSECUTION, APPELLE A L'EGLISE WALLONNE DE LEYDEN Printed by Jean le Carpentier; illus. 2 "Bull" head-pieces Given by Mrs. Nathaniel Bradford Jr. of Westchester, N. Y.
1669 1670	THE PRESENT STATE OF ENG- LAND THE FIRST PART OF THE INSTI- TUTES OF THE LAWS OF ENGLANI OR A COMMENTARY UPON LITTLETON . . . 8th ed. CAREFULLY CORRECTED Property of Joshua Thomas Esq. Plymouth. Judge Thomas was first

46

		president of The Pilgrim Society in 1820.

1670
London
Coke, Edw.

THE THIRD PART OF THE INSTI-
TUTES OF THE LAWS OF ENGLAND
. . . 4th ed. . .
Belonged to Jas. Hovey of Plimoth,
an 18th century Plymouth attorney

1670
Cambridge
Eng.
Sherringham, R.

DE ANGIORUM GENTIS ORIGINE
DESCEPTATIO . . . AUTHORE
ROBERTO SHERINGHAMO . . .
Belonged to: Wm. Brattle, 17 Nov. 1685
    Stephen Sewell
    Samuel Sevallus, April 12, 1718

1671
Coke, Edw.

THE SECOND PART OF THE
INSTITUTES OF LAWS OF
ENGLAND . . . 4th ed. . .
Belonged to James Hovey, Plymouth.
Another Copy: Belonged to Josiah
Cushing

1671
Gale, Theophilus

THEOPHILIE: OR A DISCOURSE
OF THE SAINTS AMITIE WITH
GOD IN CHRIST
Belonged to Jn° Cotton 1746

1672

THE COPIE OF A BARON'S COURT

1673
Hickes, T.

A DIALOGUE BETWEEN A
CHRISTIAN AND A QUAKER
Belonged to Josiah Cotton

1673
London
Heylyn, Peter

COSMOGRAPHIE (2 copies, w. maps)
(1) ELLINS COSMOGRAPH on spine
No title-page; damaged page w.
imprimatur, dated Whitehall, Jan. 2,
1664. The Second, Third, and Fourth
Books are dated London MDC LXXIII.
Belonged to Mrs. Lucia Knapp Royal
Given by Miss Dorothy Reed

1677
Heylyn, Peter

(2) 5th ed. corrected and enlarged by
the author. On fly-leaf, "Jn° Cushing,
his book, given by Capt. Houghton

		(who was cast away at Scituate AD 1736) for my assistance etc.
1675 Leyden	Pliny	PANEGYRICUL LIBER TRAJANO DICTUR . . .
1677	Raleigh, Walter	HISTORY OF THE WORLD IN FIVE BOOKS Given by Nathaniel Lothrop, 1826
1677	Hubbard, W.	THE PRESENT STATE OF NEW-ENGLAND, BEING A NARRATIVE OF THE TROUBLES WITH THE INDIANS . . . BY W. HUBBARD . . . LONDON: PRINTED FOR THO. PARKHURSE . . . 1677 (with map)
1677		THE MAN OF SIN or A DISCOURSE OF POPERY
1678	Calderwood, D.	HISTORY OF THE CHURCH OF SCOTLAND Title-page missing: "Brewster Bear" abd "Huntsmen" decorations Belonged to Nathaniel Russell 1820 Belonged to Catherine Elliott Russell Belonged to (Mrs. Wm. Hedge) Given by Henry R. Hedge
1678 London	de Gays, Louis	THE ART OF WAR AND THE WAY IT IS AT PRESENT PRACTICED IN FRANCE Belonged to Jn° Cushing Jr. 1727 et als
1679 London	Tonge, Ezerel	THE JESUITS MORALS OR THE PRINCIPAL ERRORS WHICH THE JESUITS HAVE INTRODUCED INTO CHRISTIAN MORALITY (front cover detached) Belonged to Sir John Cox Hippisley Lent by the Rectory, P. E. Church
1680	Baxter, Rich.	CHURCH HISTORY OF THE GOVER MENT OF BISHOPS AND COUNCIL
1681 London	Atkins	THE PRACTICK PART OF THE LAW . . .

Belonged to Thomas Lothrop
Isaac Lothrop 1726
Given by Mrs. Eunice D. Hedge

1681 London	Willis, Dr. Thomas trans. by Pordage, S.	THE REMAINING MEDICAL WORKS OF DR. THOMAS WILLIS . . . or DR. WILLISS PRACTICE OF PHYSICK Book-plate of "John Franklin, Boston, New England"
1682	Stillingfleet, Edw.	THE UNREASONABLENESS OF SEPARATISM Belonged to William Sampson, 1788
1682 London	Dalton, Michael	THE COUNTRY JUSTICE Belonged to James Warren, president of the Provincial Congress of Massa- chusetts during the American Revo- lution, friend of John Adams and husband of the noted Mercy Otis Warren
1682 London	Hooker, Richard	THE WORKS OF . . . MR RICHARD HOOKER IN EIGHT BOOKS OF ECCLESIASTICAL POLITY (damaged binding) Belonged to Timothy Davis, Wellfleet
1683 London	Cave, William	ECCLESIATICI: . . . OR THE HISTORY OF THE . . . FATHERS OF THE CHURCH . . . BY WILLIAM CAVE F. F. CHAPLAIN IN ORDINARY TO HIS MAJESTY (front cover splitting)
1683 London	Smith, John	THE MYSTERY OF RHETORIC UNVEILED Given by Mrs. Priscilla Cotton
1685 Boston		THE BOOK OF THE GENERAL LAWS OF THE INHABITANTS OF THE JURISDICTION OF NEW- PLYMOUTH . . . BY THE ORDER OF THE GENERAL COURT . . . REPRINTED AND PUBLISHED:

		NATHANIEL CLERK . . . SECR'T BOSTON IN NEW-ENGLAND: PRINTED BY SAMUEL GREEN
1685 London	Barrow, Isaac	Sermons: OF CONTENTMENT, PATIENCE, AND RESIGNATION TO THE WILL OF GOD . . . BY ISAAC BARROW, LATE MASTER OF TRINITY COLLEGE IN CAMBRIDGE From the estate of Prof. H. W. Torrey 1896
1685	Eliot, John trans.	BIBLE translated into the Indian dialect by John Eliot. Notes and signatures in Indian dialect. Given by Mrs. Wm. Cushing
1686	Burroughs	TRUE BLESSING
1667 1688	Taylor, Jeremy	SERMONS (pages up to 21 missing; front cover off) Given by Mrs. Howland, Plymouth, 1850
1683 1688 London	Smith, John	THE MYSTERY OF RHETORICK UNVEILED Given by Mrs. Priscilla Cotton
1688 Amsterdam	R. Blome	L'AMERIQUE ANGLOISE . . . AVEC DE NOUVELLES CARTES DE CHAQUE ISLES ET TERRES Traduit de l'anglaise (with maps of the West Indies, New England, New York, etc.)
1689 London	T. M. Esq.	THE OFFICE AND DUTY OF EXECUTORS Given by Mrs. Priscilla Cotton
1690 London	Dalton, Michael	THE COUNTRY JUSTICE . . . Belonged to James Otis of Barnstable, well known American Revolutionary period lawyer and defender of the rights of the American colonies.

1691 Boston, N.E.		A NARRATIVE OF THE PROCEED- INGS OF SIR EDMOND ANDROS AND HIS COMPLICES bound with THE REVOLUTION IN NEW ENGLAND JUSTIFIED . . . PRINTED FOR JOSEPH BRUNNING . . . BOSTON Belonged to Josiah Cotton
1692 London	Boyer, Peter	HISTORY OF THE VAUDOIS Belonged to John Cotton, John Cushing etc.
1694 London	Edwards, John	A DISCOURSE CONCERNING THE AUTHORITY STILE AND PER- FECTION OF THE BOOKS OF THE OLD AND NEW TESTAMENT belonged to John Cotton 1739
1696 London		THE COMPLEAT SHERIFF Belonged to Melatiah Lothrop 1746 Belonged to Isaac Lothrop
1697	Buchanan, Geo.	RERUM SCOTIARUM HISTORIA . . . (Buchanan was tutor to James I)
1646 . . . 1700 New York	R. M.	(no title-page) Argument *re* church government, *vs* Rutherford bound with: A GOSPEL ORDER REVIVED BEING AN ANSWER TO A BOOK LATELY SET FORTH BY THE REV. MR. INCREASE MATHER PRESIDENT OF HARVARD COLLEGE . . . DEDICATED TO THE CHURCHES OF CHRIST IN NEW ENGLAND (ms. note: "Printed in the Year 1700 at New York supposed to be writ by Mr. Coleman, Mr. Bradstreet, Mr. Benja. Woodbridge) Belonged to Josiah Cotton, July 6, 1702 bound with:

1668	Bres, Guy de trans. by J. S.	THE RISE, SPRING AND FOUNDA- TION OF THE ANABAPTISTS WRITTEN IN FRENCH BY GUY DE BRESE 1565 . . . and trans- lated for the use of his countrymen by J. S. Belonged to Josiah Cotton
1702 London	Mather, Cotton	MAGNALIA CHRISTI AMERICANA OR THE ECCLESTICAL HISTORY OF NEW-ENGLAND (with map) Belonged to Rev. Jos. Pickford 1795 Belonged to Samuel Wilberforce
1703		NEW-ENGLAND JUDGED BY THE SPIRIT OF THE LORD . . . FORMERI PUBLISHED BY GEORGE BISHOP AND SOMEWHAT ABBREVIATED . . . LONDON . . .
1705 London	Flavel	HUSBANDRY SPIRITUAL OR THE HEAVENLY USE OF EARTHLY THINGS Given by Mrs. Eunice D. Hedge
1705 London	Griscome	A DISCOURSE WHEREIN THE ANABAPTISTS MISSION AND MINISTRY ARE EXAMINED AND DISPROVED AND THE AX LAID TO THE ROOT OF THE TREE Belonged to John Cotton 1734 Given by Mrs. Priscilla Cotton
1707	Edwards	EVANGELICAL TRUTHS
1707 London		BIBLE – OLD TESTAMENT Belonged to Penelope, grandaughter of Josiah Winslow
1708 London	Kelying, Sir John	REPORT OF DIVERS CASES IN PLEAS OF THE CROWN . . . COLLECTED BY SIR JOHN KELYING KNT Belonged to Joshua Thomas

1709 London		THE HOLY BIBLE . . . LONDON, PRINTED BY CHARLES BELL Long owned in the Winslow family Given by Elizabeth Winslow Hayward
1712 London		ORDINES CANCELLARIAE: BEING ORDERS OF THE HIGH COURT OF CHANCERY . . . THE SECOND EDITION . . . IN THE SAVOY . . . 1712 Given by Mrs. Eunice D. Hedge
1721 Boston	Morton,Nath.	NEW-ENGLAND'S MEMORIAL . . . BY NATHANIEL MORTON . . . BOSTON . . . 1721
1722 London	Ditton, Humphrey	A DISCOURSE CONCERNING THE RESURECTION OF JESUS CHRIST Belonged to John Cushing, 1723
1725 Oxford	Dupin, L. E. trans. by Cotes, Digby	A NEW ECCLESIASTICAL HISTORY OF THE SEVENTEENTH CENTURY . . . VOLUME FIRST (it lists "Peter Martyr" as a French Calvinist author)
1726 Boston		ACTS & LAWS OF HIS MAJESTY'S PROVINCE OF THE MASSA- CHUSETTS BAY IN NEW ENGLAND . . . B. GREEN, PRINTER . . . (both covers off; pages loose) Belonged to Lieut. Cushing Jr.
1726 Boston	(Mather, Cotton)	DISCIPLINE IN THE CHURCHES IN NEW ENGLAND Belonged to Samuel Eaton
1726 Boston	Willard, Samuel	BODY OF DIVINITY (B. Green and E. Kneeland, printers) Given by T. S. Robbins, 1825
1727 London	M. LeClere	THE COMPLEAT SURGEON OR THE WHOLE ART OF SURGERY EXPLAINED (with plates) Given by James Thacher, M. D.
1788	Thomas	ENGLISH DICTIONARY

1735 London		MODERN ENTRIES IN ENGLISH BEING A CHOICE COLLECTION OF PLEADINGS IN THE COURTS OF THE KING'S BENCH . . . VOL II . . . BY A BARRISTER OF THE INNER TEMPLE . . . IN THE SAVOY
1739 London		A GENERAL ABRIDGEMENT OF CASES IN EQUITY . . . THE THIRD EDITION CORRECTED BY A GENTLEMEN OF THE MIDDLE TEMPLE IN THE SAVOY . . . 1739 Belonged to Jas. Hovey of Plim. 1754 Belonged to Joshua Thomas
1743 London	Swinburne, Henry	A TREATISE OF TESTAMENTS AND LAST WILLS . . . BY HENRY SWINBURNE . . . IN THE SAVOY . . . 1743 Belonged to Jas. Hovey of Plim. 1751 Belonged to Joshua Thomas 1800
1745 London		SUPPLEMENT TO LILLY'S PRACTI CAL REGISTER OR GENERAL ABRIDGEMENT OF THE LAW . . . IN THE SAVOY . . . 1745 Belonged to Jas. Hovey of Plim. 1751
1747	Daniel Neal	THE HISTORY OF NEW ENGLAND
1753 London	Atkinson	EPITOME OF THE ART OF NAVI- GATION . . . PRINTED FOR W. & J. MOUNT & T. PAGE
1754 London	Neal, David	THE HISTORY OF THE PURITANS . . . 2nd ed.
1755 Glasgoe	Gee, Joshua	THE TRADE AND NAVIGATION OF GREAT BRITAIN Belonged to George Atwood, 1764
1759 Boston		THE CHARTER GRANTED BY THEIR MAJESTIES KING WILLIAM AND QUEEN MARY TO THE IN- HABITANTS OF THE PROVINCE OF THE MASSACHUSETTS-BAY

		. . . BOSTON IN NEW-ENGLAND M, DCC, LIX Belonged to Col. Thomas
1760	Robbins, P.	MR. ROBBINS' SERMON AT THE ORDINATION OF HIS SON . . . BOSTON . . . 1760 (A sermon preached at the ordination of the Reverend Chandler Robbins . . . in Plymouth January 30, 1760 . . .)
1760 Boston	Robbins, P.	Another copy of the above
1764		THE LIFE OF THE REV. MR. JOHN-ATHAN EDWARDS
1768	Neal, Daniel	THE HISTORY OF NEW-ENGLAND (vol. 2) Given by Mrs. Eunice D. Hedge
1768 London	Beccaria Voltaire	AN ESSAY ON CRIMES AND PUNISHMENTS (by the Marquis Beccaria of Milan) WITH A COMMENTARY ATTRIBU-TED TO MONS. DE VOLTAIRE . . . Belonged to Wm. Thomas, James Thomas, Joshua Thomas
1769 London		THE MARINER'S NEW CALENDAR . . . LONDON PRINTED FOR J. MOUNT AND T. PAGE Belonged to: "Jonas Lucas Bot of Richard Whitworth, 1778" etc.
1772 Newport	Church, Thomas	THE ENTERTAINING HISTORY OF KING PHILIP'S WAR . . . WITH SOME ACCOUNT OF THE DIVINE PROVIDENCE TOWARD COL. BENJAMIN CHURCH: BY THOMAS CHURCH ESQ. HIS SON . . . NEWPORT . . . 1772 (title-page missing) bound with:

1772	Morton, Nathaniel	NEW ENGLAND'S MEMORIAL: . . . BY NATHANIEL MORTON . . . NEWPORT MDCCLXII
1722 Newport	Morton, Nathaniel	NEW-ENGLAND'S MEMORIAL . . . BY NATHANIEL MORTON . . . BOSTON: PRINTED NEWPORT: REPRINTED . . . M.CCLXXII
1773 Hartford	F. H. Esquire	THE RIGHT OF THE GOVERNOR AND COMPANY OF THE COLONY OF CONNECTICUT TO CLAIM . . . LANDS . . . WEST OF THE PROVIN OF NEW-YORK Belonged to Wm. Cushing
1775 Edinburgh		BIBLE . . . (old and new testament) Belonged to Wm. Bradford, 5th in descent from Gov. Bradford Given by his widow, Providence R. I.
1777	Child, Sir Josiah	A NEW DISCOURSE OF TRADE
1779 MS		COPY OF AN ORDERLY BOOK AND JOURNAL . . . MAGEBIGWEDUCE NOW CASTINE (inclosed in MS book, COMMON- WEALTH OF MASSACHUSETTS HEADQUARTERS . . . BOSTON 182
1785	Cushman, Robert	TO HIS LOVING FRIENDS . . . (Sermon preached at Plymouth, 1621 Pamphlet, dated in pencil 1785. This is the 2nd American ed.
1789		THE PERPETUAL LAW OF THE LAWS OF THE COMMONWEALTH OF MASSACHUSETTS . . . PUBLISH BY ORDER OF THE GENERAL COURT
1790	Deane, Samuel	NEW-ENGLAND FARMER Belonged to J. Warren of Plymouth who became president of the Provinci Congress of Massachusetts during the American Revolution.

1791 Portland	Freemen, Samuel	TOWN OFFICER Belonged to Thomas Davis
1722	Wilkins, John	PRINCIPLES AND DUTIES OF NATURAL RELIGION
1796 Boston	Morse, Jedidiah	AMERICAN UNIVERSAL GEOGRAPHY (maps)
1802	Freeman, Samuel	THE TOWN OFFICER . . . (fifth edition) 8vo Belonged to Charles G. Davis, Plymouth Given by Wm. T. Davis. 1899 Davis was a noted historian of Plymouth in the late 19th century.
1802 Boston	Freeman, Samuel	THE MASSACHUSETTS JUSTICE ESQ. . . Belonged to Nathaniel M. Davis, Plymouth 1807
1808 Boston	Freeman, Samuel	THE TOWN OFFICER . . . Belonged to Salisbury Jackson Plymouth 1809
1818	Dr. Goldsmith	THE GRECIAN HISTORY FROM THE EARLIEST STATE TO THE DEATH OF ALEXANDER THE GREAT
1820		(no title page) PSALMS AND HYMNS (no tunes) appears to be the church hymn-book of Nathaniel Russell, whose name is on the outside of the cover Given by Mrs. Wm. Hedge
1829	Cotton, Josiah	VOCABULARY OF THE MASSA- CHUSETTS (OR NATIC) INDIAN LANGUAGE. BY JOSIAH COTTON, CAMBRIDGE: PRINTED BY E. W. METCALF AND COMPANY. 1829 Published from the ms. of Josiah Cotton, 1680-1756

1836 Boston		THE COMPACT WITH THE CHART AND LAWS OF THE COLONY OF NEW PLYMOUTH . . . (front cover split off)
MS 1836 1844		LIST OF NAMES OF MEMBERS OF THE STANDISH GUARD APRII 1836-MAY 10, 1844 STANDISH GUARDS ORDERLY BOOK COMPANY B . . . 1844-1854
1847 Worcester	Davis, John C.	THE MASSACHUSETTS JUSTICE . (both covers split off)
1865 Boston		MOURT'S RELATION WITH INTRC DUCTION AND NOTES BY HENRY MARTIN DEXTER (with map on thin paper, including reprint of Blaskowitz map showing Plymouth Rock)
	Cushman, Robert	SERMON PREACHED IN PLYMOU IN NEW ENGLAND IN 1621
1870 Boston	Cushman, Robert	A SERMON PREACHED IN PLIMMOTH IN NEW-ENGLAND DEC. 9, 1621 . . . (fac-simile edition)
1870 Boston	Cushman, Robert	(de luxe copy of the above edition)
. . . .		BIBLE: no title-page; contains recorc of the Estes family. King James version, in black-letter from Accessio Card: "originally the property of Matthew, the Master-mariner, the first Estes who came from England. It was brought in 1723 by his younge brother, Richard the Emigrant, of John Estes, son of Matthew." '
. . . .		BIBLE: In Dutch; no title page Belonged to Mary Becket Palmer Given by George Cushman

. . . . . .
. . . . . .
BIBLE: all title pages missing;
damaged, considerable genealogical
material on Winslow family, including
list inside back cover in early hand

. . . . . . Gyffard, George
. . . . . .
FIFTEENE SERMONS UPON THE
SONG OF SALOMON . . .
Given by the Church at Plymouth
to Richard Burchard, SHIP ANNE
passenger

* . . . . . Luther, Martin
. . . . . .
A COMMENTARIE OF MASTER
DOCTOR LUTHER UPON THE
EPISTLE OF ST PAUL TO THE
GALATIANS . . .
"Martin Brewster his Book: bought
at Public Vendue at Boston June 1788"
Given by William Brewster, Kingston
*William Bradford had this title.

. . . . . .
. . . . . .
THE COPIE OF A BARONS COURT
NEWLY TRANSLATED BY WHAT-
YOU-CALL-HIM CLERK TO THE
SAME. PRINTED AT HELICON
BESIDE PARNASSUS, AND ARE
TO BE SOLD IN CALEDONIA
(verse)

1672
London
A LETTER FOR DR. ROBERT WILD
. . . TOGETHER WITH HIS
POETICA LICENTIA, A GRATULARY
POEM

1691
London
A FRIENDLY DEBATE BETWEEN
A CONFORMIST AND A NON-
CONFORMIST UPON HIS MAJESTIES
GRACIOUS DECLARATION OF
LIBERTY OF CONSCIENCE
THE DISSENTER (verse; no author
named

1704
A HYMN TO VICTORY BY THE
AUTHOR OF THE TRUE-BORN
ENGLISH-MAN (Daniel Defoe wrote
THE TRUE-BORN ENGLISH-MAN;

the Dedication to the HYMN is signed "Defoe," and there is a CONCLUSION DEDICATED to the Duke of Marlboro, signed "DF."

1704 London		FACTION DISPLAYED, A POEM
1705 Dantzick		THE DYET OF POLAND, A SATYR (verse) ms note: "By Daniel De Foe," in early hand Belonged to John Eastbury and D (?) Davis
. . . .	Dr. Southwell?	THE NEW BOOK OF MARTYRS . . . no title-page; both covers split off Is this the Elizabethan Jesuit?
. . . .	Gordon, Patrick	MODERN GEOGRAPHY (with maps No title-page; GRAMMER on spine
. . . .	Manton, Thomas	THE HUMBLE SINNER RESOLVED Given by Mrs. Wm. Hedge
. . . . . . London	Child, Sir Josiah	A NEW DISCOURSE OF TRADE . . . (4th ed. the first ed. published before 1669) "Barnabas Hedge, Jr. bought at a Vendue of Judge Olivers goods at Middleborough, Jan. 15, 1777) Given by Mrs. Eunice D. Hedge
. . . . . .	Baxter	THE REFORMED PASTOR
. . . .		A TREATISE CONCERNING SCAN Given by Mrs. Priscilla Cotton
. . . . . .		THE RISE OF THE TREATISE . . .
. . . . . .	Sewall	HYMNS
. . . .	Wolf, Jerome	DE VITA ISOCRATES . . . HIERON MUS WOLFIUS (in Latin and Greek)
. . . . . .	Wilkins, John	ON THE PRINCIPLES AND DUTIES OF NATURAL RELIGION (preface signed J. Tilottson)

Belonged to Isaac Lothrop
Given by Mrs. Eunice D. Hedge

1793	910 Morse, Jedediah	UNIVERSAL GEOGRAPHY PART II MAPS (Received 12/22/71)
1617	Brewster imprint(?)	AN ABRIDGEMENT OF THAT BOOKE WHICH THE MINISTERS OF LINCOLNE DIOCESSE DELIVERED TO HIS MAIESTIE UPON THE 1ST OF DEC. 1605 (received 12/22/71)
1644	Bernard, Richard	THESAURUS BIBLICUS SEU PROMPTUARIUM SACRUM LONDON: Felix Kingston 1644 (formerly in Essex Institute) (Received 11/29/72)
1772		PUBLII TERENTII AFRI COMOEDIAE BIRMINGHAMIAE: Johannis Baskerville (red morocco binding) (Received 12/21/72)
1630	Robert Bolton	SOME GENERAL DIRECTIONS FOR A COMFORTABLE WALKING WITH GOD London: Felix Kingston 1630 Third Edition (Received 1/15/73)
1568	Lambarde, William	ARCHAIONOMIA Ex Officine Joannis Daij 1568 (Received 1/15/73)
1518		Early Printed Specimen Leaves of John of Bromyard's SUMMA PRAEDICANTIUM Johann Stuch at Press of Anton Kobeger, Nuremberg 1518 (Received 1/15/73)

IOANNIS
CALVINI
PRÆLECTIONES:
IN
LIBRVM PROPHETIA-
RVM JEREMIÆ, ET,
LAMENTATIONES.

¶ *Joannis Budæi & Caroli Jonuillæi labore & indu-*
stria exceptæ.

Cum duobus indicibus, priore quidem rerum ac fententiarum maximè
infignium: posteriore verò locorum qui ex veteri & nouo Testa-
mento citantur, & explicantur.

GENEVÆ
APVD IO. CRISPINVM
M. D. LXIII.

PLATE 1

The firſt Decade of Sermons, written by
Henrie Bullinger.

Of the word of God, the cauſe of it, and how, and by
whom it was reuealed to the world.

The firſt Sermon.

ALl the decrees of Chriſtian faith, wyth euerie waie how to liue rightly, wel, and holily, and finally, all true and heauenly wiſdome, haue alwaies béene ſetched out of the teſtimonies oʒ determinate iudgements of the woʒd of God: neither can they, by thoſe which are wiſe men in déede, oʒ by the faithfull, and thoſe which are called by God to the miniſterie of the Churches, be dʒawn, taught, oʒ laſt of al, ſoundly confirmed from elſewhere, than out of the woʒd of God. Therefoʒe, whoſoeuer is ignoʒant what the woʒde of God, and the meaning of the woʒd of God is, hée ſéemeth to be as one, blinde, deafe, and without witte, in the Temple of the Loʒd, in the ſchoole of Chʒiſt, and laſtly, in the reading of the verie ſacred Scriptures. But whereas ſome are nothing zealous, but very hardly dʒawen to the hearing of ſermons in the Church, that ſpʒingeth out of no other fountaine than this, which is, becauſe they doe neither rightly vnderſtande, noʒ diligently inough weigh the vertue, and true foʒce of the woʒd of God. That nothing therfoʒe may cauſe the zealous beſtrers of the trueth, and the woʒde of God to ſtay on this point: but rather that that eſtimation of Gods woʒd, which is due vnto it, may be laide vp in all mens heartes, I will

(by Gods helpe) late foʒth vnto you (dearly beloued) thoſe things which a godly man ought to thinke, and holde as concerning the woʒde of God. And pʒay ye earneſtly and continually to our bountiful God, that it may pleaſe him to giue to me his holie & effectuall power to ſpeake, and to you the opening of your eares and mindes, ſo that in all that I ſhall ſaie, the Loʒde his name may be pʒaiſed, and your ſoules be pʒofited abundantly.

Firſt I haue to declare what the woʒde of God is. *Verbum* in the ſcriptures, and accoʒding to the verie pʒoperty of the Hebʒew tongue is diuerſly taken. Foʒ it ſignifieth what thing ſoeuer a man wil, euen as among the Germanes, the woʒde Ding, is moſt largely vſed. In S. Luke, the Angell of God ſaith to the bleſſed Uirgine, with God ſhall no worde be vnpoſſible, which is all one, as if he had ſaide, all things are poſſible to God, oʒ to God is nothing vnpoſſible. *Verbum* alſo ſignifieth a woʒde, vttered by the mouth of man. Sometime it is vſed foʒ a charge, ſomtime foʒ a whole ſentence oʒ ſpeach, oʒ pʒophecie: wherof in the Scriptures there are manie examples. But when *Verbum* is ioined with any thing els, as in this place we cal it *Verbū Dei*, then is it not vſed in the ſame ſigniſication. Foʒ *Verbum Dei*, the word of God, doth ſigniſie the vertue and power of God: it is alſo put foʒ the Sonne of God, which is

Verbum, what it is.

In Engliſh a thing.

The woʒd of God what it is.

A   the

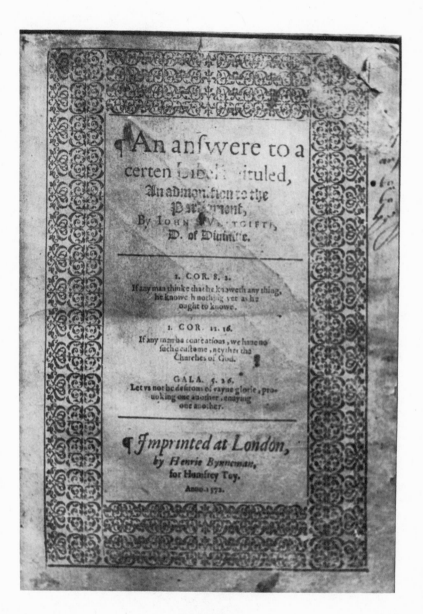

¶ An answere to a
certen libell intituled,
An admonition to the
Parliament,
By IOHN VVHITGIFT,
D. of Diuinitie.

1. COR. 8. 1.
If any man thinke that he knoweth any thing,
he knoweh h nothing yet as he
ought to knowe.

1. COR. 11. 16.
If any man be contentious, we haue no
suche custome, neyther the
Churches of God.

GALA. 5. 26.
Let vs not be desirous of vayne glorie, pro-
uoking one another, enuying
one another.

¶ Imprinted at London,
by Henrie Bynneman,
for Humfrey Toy.
Anno 1572.

PLATE 3

CONFESSIO
CHRISTIANÆ
FIDEI, ET EIVSDEM
collatio cum Papisticis
Hæresibus,

PER THEODORVM
Bezam Vezelium.

*Adiecta est altera breuis eiusdem Bezæ
fidei Confessio.*

GENEVAE,
Excudebat Eustathius Vignon
M. D. LXXVII.

PLATE 4

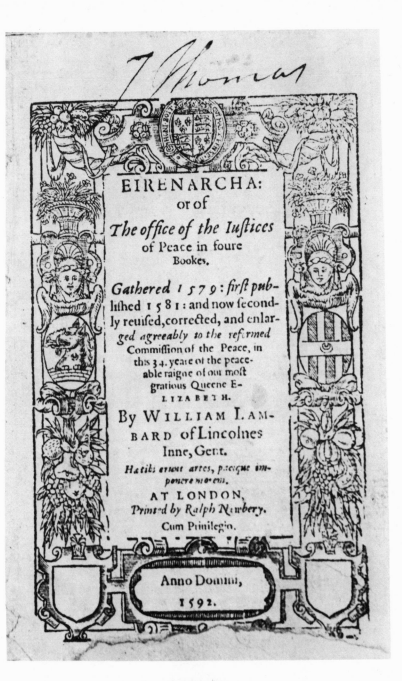

EIRENARCHA:
or of
The office of the Iustices
of Peace in foure
Bookes.

Gathered 1 5 7 9 : *first published* 1 5 8 1 : and now secondly reuised, corrected, and enlarged *agreeably to the reformed*
Commission of the Peace, in
this 3 4. yeare of the peace-
able raigne of our most
gratious Queene E-
LIZABETH.

By WILLIAM LAM-
BARD of Lincolnes
Inne, Gent.

Ha tibi erunt artes, pacique im-
ponere morem.

AT LONDON,
Printed by Ralph Newbery.
Cum Priuilegio.

Anno Domini,
1592.

PLATE 5

THE
Newe Testament
of our Lord Iesus
Chrift,

Conferred diligently with the Greeke
and beft approued tranflations
in diuers languages.

Imprinted at London by
the Deputies of Chriftopher
Barker, Printer to the Queenes
moft excellent Maieftie.
1592.

Cum gratia & priuilegio Regia Maieftatu.

PLATE 6

A
RELATION
OF THE STATE OF
Religion: and with what *Hopes and*
Pollicies it hath beene framed, and is maintained in the *severall states of these westerne*
parts of the world.

Jo: by Sandys.

LONDON,

Printed for *Simon Waterson* dwel-
ling in *Paules Churchyard* at the
signe of the Crowne.
1605

PLATE 7

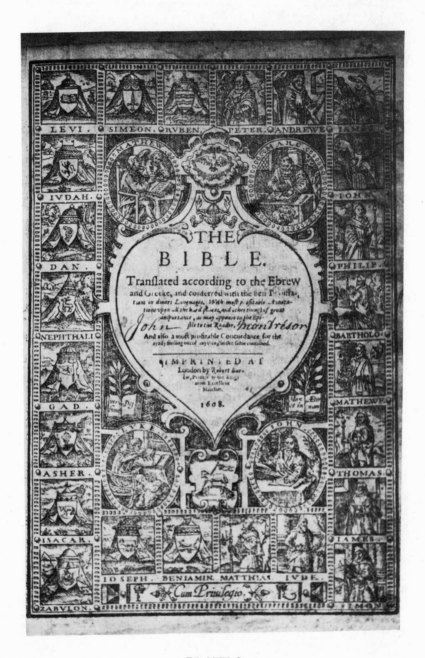

PLATE 8

THE BOOK OF
PSALMES:

Englished both in Prose
and Metre.

*With Annotations, opening the words
and sentences, by conference
with other scriptures.*

By H. A.

Ephe. 5.18.19.

*Be ye filled with the Spirit: speaking to your
selves in Psalms, and hymnes, and spiritual Songs: singing & making
melodie in your hart
to the Lord.*

Imprinted at Amsterdam,
By Giles Thorp.
A°. D. 1612.

PLATE 9

A
SECOND
MANVDVCTION,
For
Mr. ROBINSON.

Or a confirmation of the former , in an
answver to his manumission.

ANNO DOMINI.
M. *DC.* *XV.*

AN ADMONITION
TO THE PARLIAMENT

HOLDEN IN THE 13. YEARE
OF THE REIGNE OF QVEENE
ELIZABETH OF BLESSED
MEMORIE.

Begun Anno 1570. and ended 1571.

IEREM. 50. 14.

Put your selues in array against Babel round about : all you that bend your bow, shoot at her, spare no arrowes : for she hath sinned against the Lord.

IEREM. 51. 26.

They shall not take of thee a stone for a corner, nor a stone for foundation, but thou shalt be destroyed for euer.

LVKE 19. 40.

If these should hold their peace, the stones should cry.

Imprinted, Anno 1617.

PLATE 11

EEN KLARE
ENDE

Duydelijcke uytlegginghe
OVER DE

THIEN GHEBODEN
DES HEEREN·

MIDTSGADERS,

Een corte Catechismus / sommierlijck vervatende
alle de principale gronden der Christelijcker Religie.

Wtghegeven inde Enghelsche tale,
Door de Godsalighe ende VVel-gheleerde

Mr. IOHAN DOD, ende ROBERT CLEAVER

Wt de Enghelsche in onse Neder-duytsche Tale
ghetrouwelijck overgheset
D O O R
VINCENTIVM MEVSEVOET,
Bedienaer des Heylighen Euangelij tot Schaghen.

TOT LEYDEN,
Voor Guiliaem Brewster / Boeck-drucker.
Anno 1617.

PLATE 12

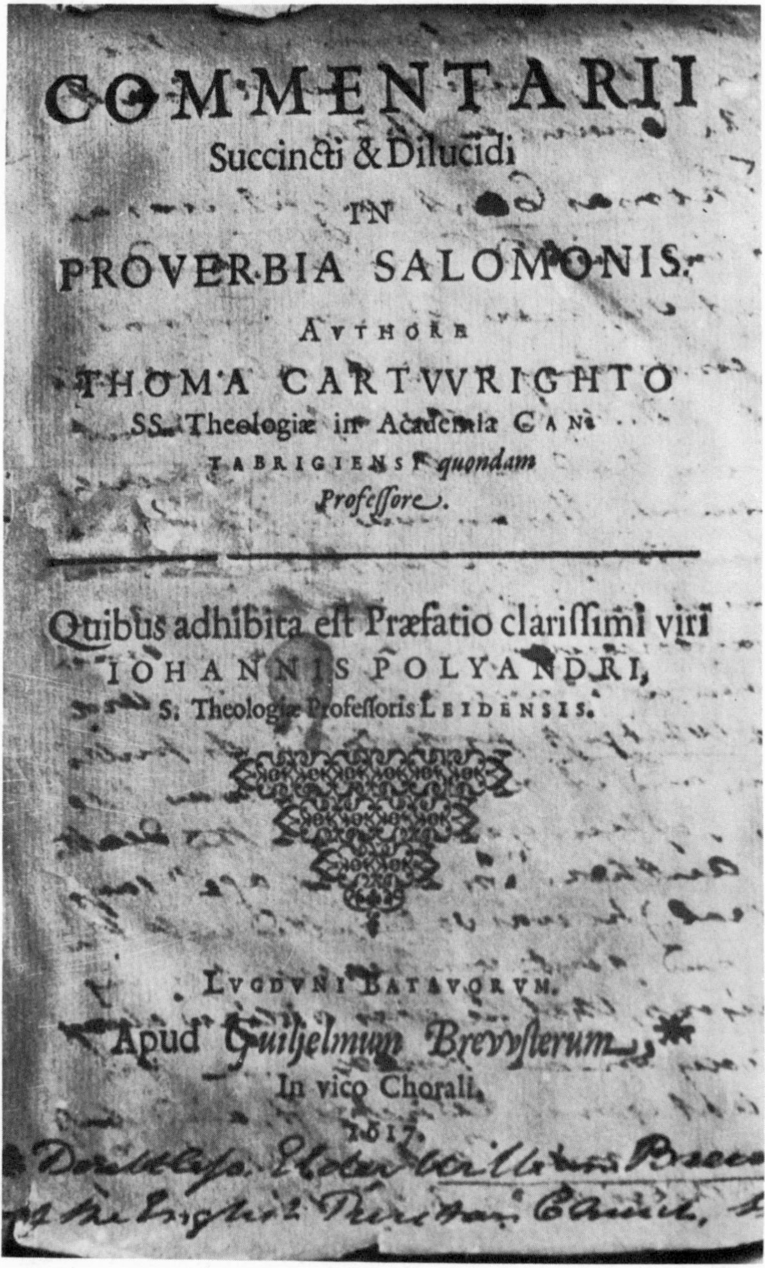

COMMENTARII

Succincti & Dilucidi

IN

PROVERBIA SALOMONIS.

AVTHORE

THOMA CARTVVRIGHTO

SS. Theologiæ in Academia CAN-

TABRIGIENSI *quondam*

Professore.

Quibus adhibita est Præfatio clarissimi viri

IOHANNIS POLYANDRI,

S. Theologiæ Professoris LEIDENSIS.

LVGDVNI BATAVORVM.

Apud *Guilielmum Brewsterum*

In vico Chorali.

1617.

Doctissa Elder William Brewster of the English Puritan Church

---

PLATE 13

GVIL. AMESII

ad · Responsum

NIC. GREVINCHOVII

RESCRIPTIO

CONTRACTA.

*Accedunt ejusdem assertiones
Theologicæ de Lumine
Naturæ & Gra-
tiæ.*

Proſtant
LVGDVNI BATAVORVM,
Apud Guiljelmum Brewſterum
In Vico Chorali,
1617,

PLATE 14

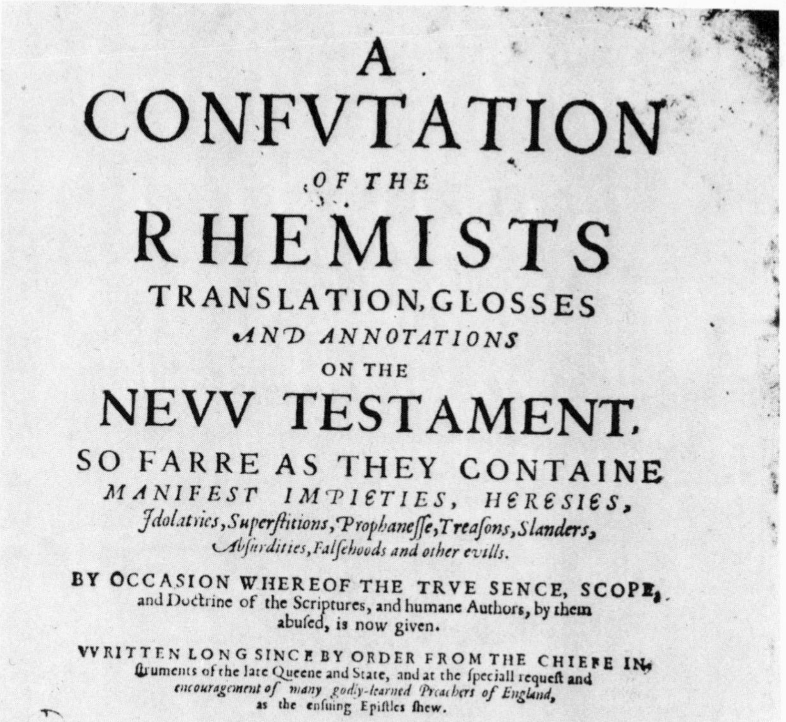
A
CONFVTATION
OF THE
RHEMISTS
TRANSLATION, GLOSSES
AND ANNOTATIONS
ON THE
NEVV TESTAMENT.
SO FARRE AS THEY CONTAINE
MANIFEST IMPIETIES, HERESIES,
Idolatries, Superstitions, Prophanesse, Treasons, Slanders,
Absurdities, Falsehoods and other evills.

BY OCCASION WHEREOF THE TRVE SENCE, SCOPE, and Doctrine of the Scriptures, and humane Authors, by them abused, is now given.

VVRITTEN LONG SINCE BY ORDER FROM THE CHIEFE INstruments of the late Queene and State, and at the speciall request and *encouragement of many godly-learned Preachers of England,* as the ensuing Epistles shew.

By that Reverend, Learned, and Iudicious Divine,
THOMAS CARTVVRIGHT,
sometime Divinitie Reader of
Cambridge.

Worth.

Joh Worth

Printed in the yeare 1618.

PLATE 15

DE
REGIMINE
ECCLESIÆ
SCOTICANÆ
BREVIS RE-
LATIO.

Impreſſus Anno Dom.
1618.

PLATE 16

PERTH
ASSEMBLY.

CONTAINING

1. The Proceedings thereof.
2. The Proofe of the Nullitie thereof.
3. Reasons presented thereto against the receiving the fiue new *Articles* imposed.
4. The oppositenesse of it to the proceedings and oath of the whole state of the Land. *An.*1581.
5. Proofes of the unlawfulnesse of the said fiue Articles, *viz.* 1. Kneeling in the act of Receiving the Lords Supper. 2. Holy daies. 3. Bishopping. 4. Private Baptisme. 5. Private Communion.

EXOD. 20. 7.

Thou shalt not take the name of the Lord thy God in vaine, for the Lord will not hold him guiltlesse that taketh his name in vaine.

COLOS. 2. 8.

Beware lest there be any that spoyle you through Philosophy & vain deceit, through the traditions of men, according to the rudiments of the World, and not of Christ.

MDCXIX.

PLATE 17

Charles Chauncy 1734

❁ ✳✳✳✳✳✳✳✳✳ ❁

ANNOTATIONS
UPON THE FOURTH BOOK
OF MOSES, *CALLED*

NUMBERS.

WHEREIN, BY CONFERENCE OF THE
SCRIPTVRES, BY COMPARING THE GREEK AND
Chaldee Verſions, and teſtimonies of Hebrew writers;
the Lawes and Ordinances given of old unto
Iſrael in this book, are explained.

By *Henry Ainſworth.*

I Will put you in remembrance, though ye once knew this, how that
the Lord having ſaved a people out of the land of Egypt, afterward de-
ſtroyed them that beleeved not. Iude v. 5.

Fourtie yeres was I grieved with this generation. Pſal. 95. 10.

But with whom was he grieved fourtie yeres? was it not with them that
had ſynned, whoſe carkeſſes fell in the wildernes? And to whom ſware he,
that they ſhould not enter into his reſt; but to them that beleeved not? So
wee ſee, that they could not enter in, becauſe of unbeleef. Let us
labour therfore to enter into that Reſt, leſt any man
fall after the ſame example of unbeleef.
Heb. 3. 17. 18. 19. & 4. 11.

Iſrael ❁ ❁ ❁ *Stoughton*
Imprinted in the yere 1619.

PLATE 18

* * *

ANNOTATIONS
Upon the first book of Moses,
called

GENESIS.

Wherein the Hebrew words and sentences, are compared with,
explained by the ancient Greek and Chaldee versions:
but chiefly, by conference with the
holy Scriptures.

By H. A.

Moses *commanded us a Law* ; *the inheritance of the*
Church of Iakob. Deut. 33. 4.
Remember the Law, of Moses my servant : which I com-
manded him in Horeb, for all Israel ; *with the Statutes*
and Iudgments. Malach. 4. 4.

* * *
* *
*

Imprinted in the yeare
1 6 2 1.

PLATE 19

RELATION OR

Iournall of the beginning and proceedings
of the English Plantation setled at *Plimoth* in N E W
E N G L A N D, by certaine English Aduenturers both
Merchants and others.

With their difficult passage, their safe ariuall, their
ioyfull building of, and comfortable planting them-
selues in the now well defended Towne
of N E W P L I M O T H.

AS ALSO A RELATION OF FOVRE
seuerall discoueries since made by some of the
same English Planters there resident.

I. *In a iourney to* P V C K A N O K I C K *the habitation of the Indians greatest King* Massasoyt : *as also their message, the answer and entertainment
they had of him.*

I I. *In a voyage made by ten of them to the Kingdome of* Nawset, *to seeke
a boy that had lost himselfe in the woods : with such accidents as befell them
in that voyage.*

I I I. *In their iourney to the Kingdome of* Namaschet, *in defence of their
greatest King* Massasoyt, *against the* Narrohiggonsets, *and to reuenge the
supposed death of their Interpreter* Tisquantum.

I I I I. *Their voyage to the* Massachusets, *and their entertainment there.*

With an answer to all such obiections as are any way made
against the lawfulnesse of English plantations
in those parts.

LONDON,
Printed for *Iohn Bellamie*, and are to be sold at his shop at the two
Greyhounds in Cornhill neere the Royall Exchange. 1622.

PLATE 20

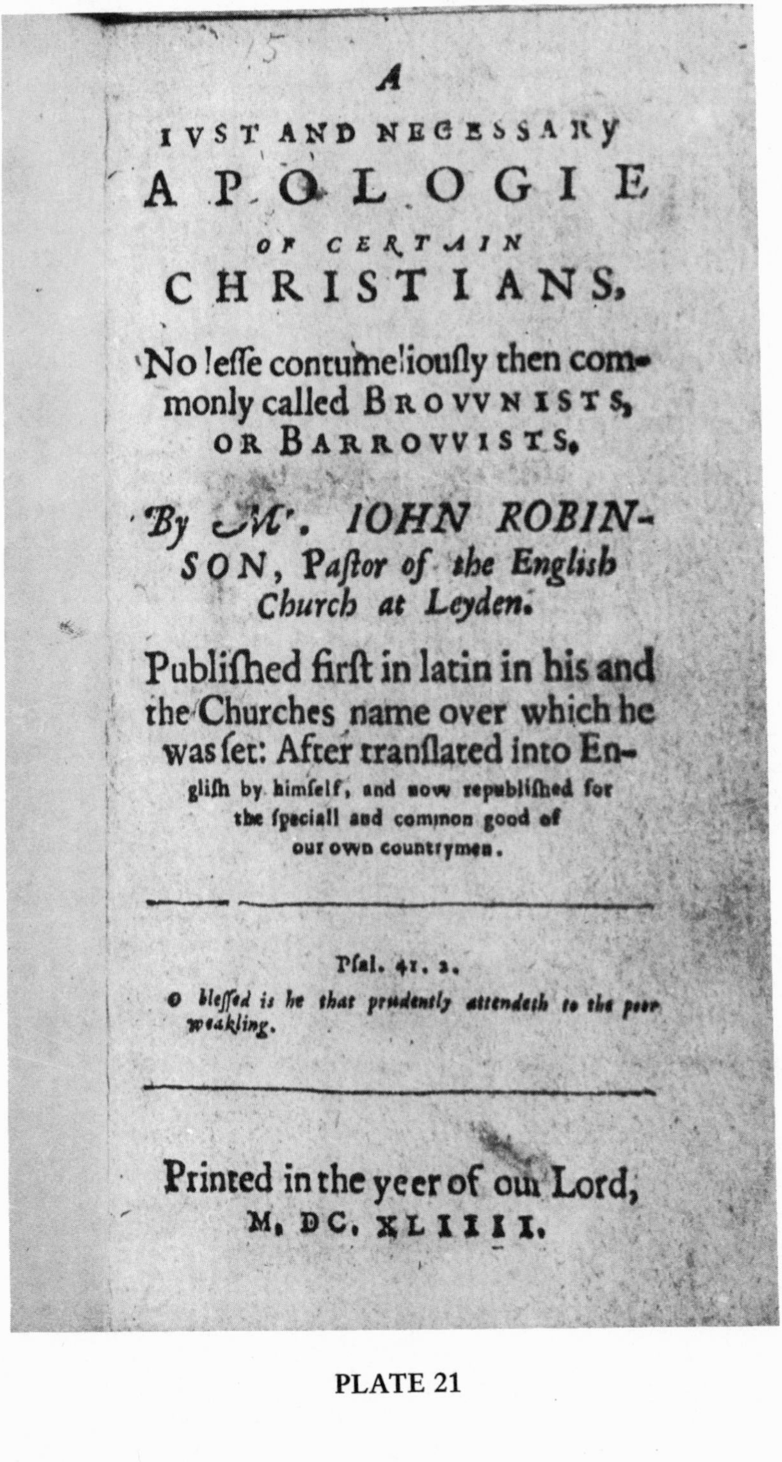

A
IVST AND NECESSARY
APOLOGIE
OF CERTAIN
CHRISTIANS,

No leſſe contumeliouſly then commonly called BROVVNISTS,
OR BARROVVISTS.

By M. *IOHN ROBIN-*
SON, Paſtor of the Engliſh
Church at Leyden.

Publiſhed firſt in latin in his and
the Churches name over which he
was ſet: After tranſlated into Engliſh by himſelf, and now republiſhed for
the ſpeciall and common good of
our own countrymen.

Pſal. 41. 2.

O bleſſed is he that prudently attendeth to the poor
weakling.

Printed in the yeer of our Lord,
M. DC. XLIIII.

PLATE 21

ESSAYES;

OR,

OBSERVATIONS

DIVINE AND MORALL.

COLLECTED OVT OF

holy Scriptures, Ancient and
Moderne Writers, both di-
vine and humane.

As also, out of the great volume
of mens manners: Tending to the
furtherance of knowledge
and vertue.

By IOHN ROBINSON.

The second Edition, with two Tables, the one of
the Authours quoted; The other of the matters contained in the Observations.

PROVERBS 9.9:
Give instruction to a wise man, and he will be wiser,
teach a Righteous man, and hee will increase in lear-
ning.

LONDON,
Printed by *I. D.* for *I. Bellamie*, at the
three golden Lyons in Cornhill neere
the Royall Exchange. 1638.

PLATE 22

Hypocrisie Unmasked:

BY

A true Relation of the Proceedings of the Governour and Company of the *Massachusets* against Samvel Gorton (and his Accomplices) a notorious disturber of the Peace and quiet of the severall Governments wherein he lived : With the grounds and reasons thereof, examined and allowed by their Generall Court holden at *Boston* in *New-England* in *November* last, 1646.

Together with a particular Answer to the manifold slanders, and abominable falshoods which are contained in a Book written by the said *GORTON*, and entituled, *Simplicities defence against Seven-headed Policy, &c.*

DISCOVERING

To the view of all whose eyes are open, his manifold Blasphemies; As also the dangerous agreement which he and his Accomplices made with ambitious and treacherous *Indians*, who at the same time were deeply engaged in a desperate Conspiracy to cut off all the rest of the *English* in the other Plantations.

VVhereunto is added a briefe Narration (occasioned by certain aspersions) of the true grounds or cause of the first Planting of *New-England*; the President of their Churches in the way and Worship of God; their Communion with the *Reformed Churches* ; and their practise towards those that dissent from them in matters of Religion and Church-Government.

By *Edw. Winslow.*

Psal. 120.3. *What shall be given unto thee, or what shall be done unto thee thou false tongue ?*
Vers. 4. *Sharpe arrows of the Mighty, with coales of Juniper.*

Published by *Authority.*

London, Printed by *Rich. Cotes* for *John Bellamy* at the three Golden Lions in *Cornhill*, neare the Royall Exchange, 1646.

PLATE 23

NEW-ENGLANDS
MEMORIALL:
OR,

A brief Relation of the moſt Memorable and Remarkable
Paſſages of the Providence of God, manifeſted to the

PLANTERS
OF
New-England in *America;*

With ſpecial Reference to the firſt Colony thereof, Called
NEW-PLIMOUTH.

As alſo a Nomination of divers of the moſt Eminent Inſtruments
deceaſed, both of Church and Common-wealth, improved in the
firſt beginning and after-progreſs of ſundry of the reſpective
Juriſdictions in thoſe Parts; in reference unto ſundry
Exemplary Paſſages of their LIVES, and
the time of their DEATH.

Publiſhed for the Uſe and Benefit of preſent and future Generations,
By *NATHANIEL MORTON,*
Secretary to the Court for the Juriſdiction of *New-Plimouth.*

Deut. 32.10. *He found him in a deſert Land, in the waſte howling wilderneſs he led him*
about; he inſtructed him, he kept him as the Apple of his Eye.
Jerem. 2.2,3. *I remember thee, the kindneſs of thy youth, the love of thine Eſpouſals,*
when thou wenteſt after me in the wilderneſs, in a Land that was not ſown,&c.
Deut. 8. 2,16. *And thou ſhalt remember all the way which the Lord thy God led thee*
this FORTY YEARS in the wilderneſs, &c.

CAMBRIDGE:
Printed by *S.G.* and *M.J.* for *John Uſher* of *Boſton.* 1669.

PLATE 24

NOTES ON THE PLATES

No. 1
1563
The Commentaries of John Calvin on the Book of the Prophecies of Jeremiah, and the Lamentations. Obtained by the labor and industry of John Budaeus and Charles Jonuillaeus. With two indices, the first of the most important subjects and concepts; but the second, of the places which are cited from the Old and New Testaments, and are explained. (Geneva, 1563). One of many reformed biblical commentaries available to the Pilgrims. Elder Brewster had Calvin's commentaries on Daniel, Ezekiel, and Isaiah.

No. 2
c. 1550
Henrie or Heinrich Bullinger (1504-1575) served as "People's Priest of Zurich" from 1531 until his death in 1575 during which time he produced "Fiftie Godlie and Learned Sermons, devided into five Decades, Conteyning the Chief and Principall Pointes of Christian Religion." This is a page from the first sermon in the first volume of the series.

No. 3
1572
John Whitgift (1530-1604), Archbishop of Canterbury was a mighty antagonist of the Puritan party. From 1583 to 1604 as Archbishop he accelerated first Elizabeth's and then James' hostility to the Puritans. This Answere To A Certain Libel was in response to An Admonition To The Parliament written in 1572 by two London ministers, John Field and Thomas Wilcox, advocates of the Presbyterian system.

No. 4
1577
A Confession of the Christian Faith, and the Comparison of it With the Papist Heresies by Theodore Beza Vezelius. Appended also is another short confession of faith by the same Beza. (Geneva, 1577). Beza (1519-1605) was in many ways the theological successor to Calvin at Geneva. His works also found their way into Brewster's library.

No. 5
1592
William Lambarde's Eirenarcha (1592) descended in the possession of the trial justices of Plymouth until it was deposited in Pilgrim Hall by the last Justice, Arthur Lord c. 1915. The cover has the arms of William Cecil, Lord Burghley. It is thought that the book may have arrived in Plymouth by way of Davison, secretary to

Lord Burghley and patron of William Brewster. At least the 1592 edition of *Eirenarcha* has been missing from the shelves of the Burghley library for quite some time. The title page displays the signature of Joshua Thomas, Trial Justice at the turn of the 18th century and one of the founders of the Pilgrim Society.

No. 6
1592

This is the New Testament frontispiece of the Bible belonging to Governor William Bradford, the 1592 Geneva edition known as the "Breeches Bible" because of the use of "breeches" for "aprons" in Genesis 3:7. Barely perceptible is the signature of Chloe Bradford, great granddaughter of the Governor. It came to the Pilgrim Society in 1903.

No. 7
1605

Sir Edwyn Sandys, author of this *Relation* was a son of the Bishop of York and a member of the Council of the Virginia Company. In both relations he had close association with William Brewster who, before his flight to Holland, was in the employ of the Sandys family at Scrooby. The frontispiece is of even more particular interest because it bears one of the rare autographs of John Robinson.

No. 8
1608

Robert Barker's 1608 "black letter" edition of the Bible with the signature of an unidentified "John Montreson."

No. 9
1612

Henry Ainsworth (1571-1623) is represented in Plymouth inventories by his Psalters and Commentaries. In the twenty-one Wills and Inventories filed between 1633 and 1640 at Plymouth, eleven mention books among which are six psalters. Dr. Samuel Fuller of the Mayflower had one of these, probably the Amsterdam edition of Ainsworth. Rose T. Briggs identifies this as the volume in Longfellow's "Courtship of Myles Standish" on Priscilla Mullins' lap:

> Open wide on her lap lay the well-worn
> psalm book of Ainsworth,
> Printed in Amsterdam, the words and music
> together,
> Rough-hewn angular notes, like stones in the
> wall of a church-yard,
> Darkened and overhung by the running vine of
> the verses.

No. 10
1615

This *Second Manvdvction For Mr. Robinson* was written by William Ames to the Pilgrim pastor John Robinson in 1615 in response to Robinson's response (*A Manvmission to a Manvdvction*) of the same year to Ames' *A Manvdvction For Mr. Robinson, and such as Consent with him in Privat Communion, To Lead them on to Publick* (1614). Ames and Robinson agreed on many things, but not on the organization of a church. Both able disputants, Robinson mocked Ames by a pun on his name, calling him "Dr. Amiss," and Ames, furious, replied with a scolding letter, the first of these exchanges. Robinson accepted the rebuke.

No. 11
1617

John Field and Thomas Wilcox produced this strongly worded *Admonition* in 1572 which advocated the extreme Presbyterian polity of Thomas Cartwright. In that same year, Cartwright was deprived of his Cambridge Fellowship and John Whitgift made spirited reply to the work of Field and Wilcox by his *Answere To A Certain Libel* (see No. 3).

No. 12
1617

A Plaine And Familiar Exposition of the Ten Commandments of God by John Dod and Robert Cleaver (Leyden, 1617). Printed in English and Dutch, by Elder William Brewster, four copies were recorded in Plymouth inventories: Brewster's in Dutch, and three in English, belonging to Dr. Fuller, the Godbertsons, and Governor Bradford.

No. 13
1617

Concise And Clear Commentaries On The Proverbs of Solomon, by the Author Thomas Cartwright, Formerly A Professor of Holy Theology In the College of Cambridge. To Which is appended a preface of the most eminent man, John Polyander, Professor of Holy Theology At Leyden. Another Brewster imprint of great importance, this represents the work of Thomas Cartwright (1535-1603). While Lady Margaret Professor of Divinity at Cambridge in 1569, he urged Presbyterian practice upon the English Church and was deprived first of his professorship and then of his fellowship at the instigation of John Whitgift in 1672.

No. 14
1617

An Answer Of William Ames Given To the Response of Nicholas Grevinchovius. The Theological Assertions

Concerning the Light of Nature and Grace Are Added.
(Leyden, 1617). Ames (1576-1633) was a prominent
English Puritan theologian living in Holland. Noted as an
able combatant in the Dutch theological controversies,
he had since 1613 been engaged in a lengthy dispute
with Nicholas Grenvichovius, famous Remonstrant
pastor at Rotterdam. In 1617, Brewster printed this and
*Rescriptio Scholastice brevis ad. Nicol. Grevinchvoii
responsum illud prolizum etc.* (Brief Scholastic reply to
that Prolix Response of Nich. Grevinchoven, etc.) on his
illegal Choir Alley Press at Leyden.

No. 15   The Rhemist translation which provoked this confuta-
1618   tion by Dr. Cartwright was the result of the Roman
          Catholic Church's desire to translate the bible into the
          vernacular "for the speedy abolishing . . . of false and
          impious translations put forth by sundry sects." The
          New Testament translation was done in 1582 in the
          English College at Rheimes, and the Old Testament at
          Douai in 1609-1610. Cartwright began his work when
          the translation appeared in 1582 and devoted the rest of
          his life to it; at that he did not live to finish it or (as his
          publisher says to the studious reader) "survey so
          accurately as otherwise he would all the quotations of
          ancient writers which he had occasion to mention." He
          got as far as the fifteenth chapter of Revelation, all in all
          some 761 pages of text.

No. 16   *A Brief Relation About the Governing of the Scottish
1618   Church* (1618) and

No. 17   *Perth Assembly* (1619). The publication of these two
1618   books by William Brewster on the Pilgrim Press at Choir
          Alley led to the suppression of the press and a great
          hunt after William Brewster. David Calderwood
          (1560-1625) was the author of these two works
          vigorously opposed to episcopacy in Scotland. Charles I
          bitterly resented these attacks upon the Scottish settle-
          ment. The full account of the efforts at suppression is
          contained in Edward Arber's *The Story of The Pilgrim
          Fathers, 1606-1623* (London, 1897).

No. 18   Ainsworth was the teacher of the Separatist congre-
1619   gation at Amsterdam, and in 1619, published these

No. 19
1621
Annotations or commentaries upon the book of Numbers. The Pilgrim Society also owns his Annotations upon Genesis, Exodus, Leviticus, Psalms, and Song of Songs. His works are represented in the inventories of Samuel Fuller, William Brewster, John Jenney, and Richard Langford.

No. 20
1622
Frontispiece of the so-called "Mourt's Relation" (1622).

No. 21
1644
(1625)
John Robinson (1576-1625) was the pastor of the Pilgrim Separatist Church at Leyden and their chief mentor. Of him Bradford in his *Dialogues* says in part, "As he was a man learned and of solid judgement, and of a quick and sharp wit, so was he also of a tender conscience, and very sincere in all his ways . . . He was an acute and expert disputant, very quick and ready, and had much bickering with the Arminians, . . . He was very profitable in his ministry and comfortable to his people." (Young's *Chronicles*, p. 452.) This is the third (1644) edition of the *Apology*, the second in English. It was first published in Latin in 1619, and in English in 1625, the year of his death.

No. 22
1638
Robinson's *Essayes* saw two editions, 1625 and 1638, both of which are represented in the Library of the Pilgrim Society. Rather than weighty theological disputations, these essays tend to be rather homely observations on a wide variety of issues.

No. 23
1646
Frontispiece of Winslow's *Hypocrisie Unmasked* (1646).

No. 24
1669
Frontispiece of Nathaniel Morton's *New England's Memorial* (1669).

This publication has been typeset in a 12 point Aldine Roman face. The type is designed after that of the Italian printer, Aldus Manutius, a Classical Scholar and friend of Erasmus of Rotterdam. Aldus founded the Aldine Press in 1494 in Venice. He employed Francesco Griffo of Bologna, an independent punch cutter, to produce the Aldine font that bears his name. Italics were first designed by the Aldine Press in 1501. The type for this book has been set by Stanley Cobb of Pilgrim Publishers of Kingston, Massachusetts. The book was printed and bound in Ann Arbor, Michigan.

Device of Aldus Manutius